"Making the complex simple is really hard – especially when you're in the midst of things as a leader. This brilliant book does just that. It's a 'go to' for me if I need to step out and re-set my perspective in order to move things forwards."

KATE COLLINS – CEO, TEENAGE CANCER TRUST

"David Mansfield tells it like is...and how work and life can and should be better. We don't half complicate things! I know from experience David doesn't do waffle and I wish he'd written this no-nonsense and no-jargon book years ago."

GERRY MURPHY – CHAIRMAN, BURBERRY PLC

"Less a business book and more a series of captivating stories that give brilliant lessons for being more effective and successful at work. A fantastic page turning read!"

BRUCE DAISLEY – UK PRESIDENT, TWITTER

"David Mansfield was always known as a tough operator from his earliest days in TV. He is also known for building strong teams, who share a unified vision and have a lot of fun. His range of experience written in his inimitable, no-nonsense, dry style will make this a very readable and useful book."

DAME CAROLYN McCALL – CEO ITV PLC

"Delightfully waspish and witty, punchy and practical. A "just get it done" manifesto for our over-complicated, jargonistic business times. A must-read."

ROBERT PHILIPPS – FOUNDER, JERICHO CHAMBERS

"If *The Monday Revolution* was a private members club I'd join!"
– FOUNDER, SOHO HOUSE

T0284705

"What an invaluable book. With many real life examples, it is packed full of useful tips to give tangible and long lasting results, and improve the performance of your business. Setting this out in the context of a taking control of your working week is a nice touch."

ANDREW WILKES – PARTNER, SMITH & WILLIAMSON

"At Capital we kept Manno away from the music but he did his best to keep me away from the money!!"

CHRIS TARRANT – TV PERSONALITY

"It's very rare to find a business book that is a real page turner, the Monday Revolution is one of them. All too often, business books are written with little context, but the real-world stories David provides throughout this book, help provide great examples of how to (or how not to) put the advice into action. A must read for any CEO/Entrepreneur interested in a very comprehensive guide to operating at the highest level."

PAUL THOMAS – CEO, LEAD FORENSICS

"Being on a board and working with David was fun, whilst the serious side of business got done. Read this book and have fun while absorbing the serious matter."

PETER WILLIAMS – CHAIRMAN, SUPERDRY PLC

"Building a business is relentless hard work, and you are supposed to have all the answers all the time – and of course you don't. That's why you need David, and if you can't get him, then get his book. He is smart, highly commercial, direct, uncompromising and, annoyingly, usually right. Keep this book by your desk and use it regularly. Its great advice, but not always easy to implement – but then building a business isn't easy."

ANDREW GRANT – FOUNDER, TULCHAN
COMMUNICATIONS LLP

"Packed with stories, case studies and immediate actions you can take NOW, this book is a must read, whether you're running an established company or building a new enterprise."

PAUL LINDLEY – FOUNDER, ELLA'S KITCHEN

"You could spend your life savings on business books by celebrity authors and academics building their reputation. This one is different. It's a candid digest of supremely practical reflections by a highly effective leader with nothing to prove. I recommend it to you."

RICHARD EYRE – CHAIRMAN, NEXT 15 PLC

"Journeys start with steps, weeks start with days. Mondays are often tough, this book helps you make them your friend, not foe. It's time to #LoveMonday"

WILL KING – FOUNDER, KING OF SHAVES.

"In *The Monday Revolution* David advises 'hanging out with the right people pays dividends'. I hung out with David for many years and relished being the fortunate recipient of a multitude of his lessons. Dividends can be achieved for anyone interested in business by simply reading this book.

The Monday Revolution is a reflection of David's inspiring, wise, humorous and music loving character. It's a brilliant precis of the best business lessons and applicable to any sector, at any time.

The Monday Revolution is the best business short-cut; take it. Business people consistently fall into the same pitfalls, experience and mistakes are seemingly the best way to learn, until now! Learn business lessons the easy way – read David's book."

MARTINA KING – CEO, FEATURE SPACE

"This isn't just a helpful book about business; it's a helpful book about life."

KEITH REID – LYRIST, 'A WHITER SHADE OF PALE'

"David Mansfield has been a sharp and insightful business leader, advisor and commentator in a multitude of environment over many years. In *The Monday Revolution*, his humanity, humour and pragmatism are combined with his commercial savvy and business acumen so that all can benefit from his cleverly and clearly written suggestions. With the excellent, action-oriented summaries at the end of each chapter, I challenge anyone to come away from *The Monday Revolution* without a bag full of helpful new ways of conducting their daily life."

WILLIAM ALEXANDER – CONSULTANT,
SPENCER STUART

"I have benefited from David's wise words many times over the years, even if I haven't always wanted to hear them. This book is full of useful lessons on business and life. Roll on *The Monday Revolution*."

JAMES CLAYTON – FILM PRODUCER, CHAIRMAN,
BEANO STUDIOS

THE
MONDAY
REVOLUTION

SEIZE CONTROL OF
YOUR BUSINESS LIFE

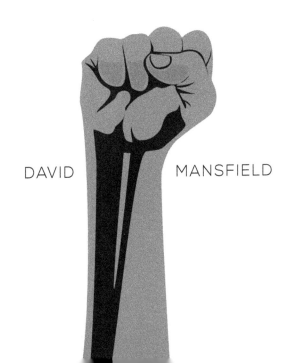

DAVID   MANSFIELD

First published in Great Britain by Practical Inspiration
Publishing, 2020

© David Mansfield, 2020

The moral rights of the author have been asserted

ISBN   978-1-78860-148-1 (print)
        978-1-78860-147-4 (epub)
        978-1-78860-146-7 (mobi)

Practical Inspiration
PUBLISHING

Contents

Introducing *The Monday Revolution*

Liberation! Freedom from the shackles of mundane mediocrity! There's no bloodshed involved here but there will be metaphorical battles fought. Because your personal revolution will challenge the established way of getting things done. You've had enough of the way things are in your business life and you're going to revolutionise the working week.

Your revolution is, in many respects, a silent one you've decided to adopt as your own special way of effective working. You will need to develop your own tailor-made revolution appropriate to your own situation and circumstances. There's no particular need to share the fact you're on a mission of improvement and change.

The Monday Revolution could significantly change your business life. There are limitless opportunities to raise your game and that of your organisation, but where to start? *The Monday Revolution* outlines simple ways of cutting through everyday challenges to achieve immediate results. Of course, it's not a repair manual and you'll need to work out how to apply the case studies and examples relative to where you work and what you do. But do that and the results will be liberating!

I can't tell you exactly what to do on Monday – that would be too prescriptive. But I can help your approach to the working week with practical day-to-day and longer-term strategic advice. This should provide a valuable complement to the financial tools you employ as part of running your business life. Shared experiences, which I think you'll relate to, will act as a prompt to take action.

In order to implement *The Monday Revolution*, I've assumed you have a certain level of authority and control. We're probably talking, in conventional terms, senior manager to chief executive, chairman or owner and all points in between. Otherwise, I sense I might provoke a sense of frustration from those who agree with the ideas but feel powerless to move things forward.

However, if you've not yet succeeded in attaining the levels of responsibility some of the examples require, not to worry. Park the ideas until you're ready and you'll start off in the right way. It's much better than trying to change something you've put in place that already needs fixing.

Revolutionaries are self-disciplined and focused on the final result. To that end, apply the principles that run through this book. You'll recognise them in the many stories and anecdotes as the chapters unfold.

- *Invest time wisely.* It's always in short supply and not easily stored for another day. An invaluable resource. The revolutionary spends their time on the right things each week to improve the chances of effective results and maximum satisfaction.
- *Find better ways.* Around you there are many examples of better ways to solve your own problems and create compelling opportunities. Learn to look outside.
- *Simple, not complicated.* Revolutionaries are mission clear. Too many moving parts and you'll increase the chance of failure. Avoid the trap of trying to solve

complex problems with complex solutions. Whatever you're doing or saying, keep it simple.

- *Now, not later.* The enemy of effective working is procrastination. What is wrong with now?
- *Evidence-based decision making.* Sometimes there will be little to go on. But this is rare. More likely, the facts are there, but overruled by emotions. Be strong. Look for evidence to back up decisions. Before you decide, how do you really know?
- *Positive mindset.* Revolutionaries never win without belief. Neither will you.

The Monday Revolution is a state of mind to apply on the first day of the week. It's a metaphor for recognising that some things need to change now. It's an approach that relies on simple steps to achieve smart ways of getting things done, immediately.

The business world is complex and that's not going to stop anytime soon. The ever-increasing supply of information, disruptive competition and growing demands on executive time point to a different approach to organising and running a company. Traditional ways of operating are simply no longer good enough.

Change rarely suddenly arrives. It's a constant. The pace may vary but it never stops. Recognition and acknowledgement are the drivers of action, which is about taking control and building those challenges into your daily routine. It's a rocky journey where you never arrive at the destination. But that's why life is exciting. In the early part of my business career, I used to think all I needed to do was deal with the current challenges and some form of steady state would kick in. After a few years, I realised that was the steady state! Constant disruption and left-field moments to sort out are part of the way strong companies are built. They become part of the business DNA.

Changing an organisation from the middle, or even the upper, ranks is no easy task. Yet, there are steps to take which can significantly improve productivity, the working day and the satisfaction of going to work. Evolution is how the world has developed over millions of years. But we haven't got that long. There's a good chance your working model is broken in many places and will require a more radical approach if things are to change for the better.

And that's *The Monday Revolution*.

I've worked at and with many businesses, big and small. Some incredibly successful, some not so and some that went bust. In what has been a long life of learning I've concluded that simple things done well are more rewarding and definitely more effective. Long-term planning, processes and approvals have their place, but not at the expense of immediate improvement and an ability to look forward to the working week. For me there's a good test: it's how you feel on Sunday evening when you think about the days in front of you.

And too often the week is a congested mess of internal and external meetings of little direct relevance. Or tasks that make a limited contribution to the company's or your own advancement. Yet there they are, sitting in your calendar, a depressing reminder of what's in store.

I remember that playing for the school football team meant you always escaped double physics (the teacher, not the subject, was the problem) at least twice a month. Unfortunately, I didn't make the cut so double physics it was. And that's how many people feel on the eve of their working week. Not enough bright spots and too many things to just get through. Not enjoying their week but enduring it. But it doesn't have to be like that. With a positive mind and some new ideas, it's possible to become a better, more effective person. And that means being more satisfied and happier too – which ultimately is what we all want to achieve. Life is far too short to spend it looking back wondering why we didn't change our ways sooner.

The Monday Revolution is about changing your personal approach to work and life. It's about taking control of time and spending it on the things that matter. There is great satisfaction in getting things done. Who wants to spend long days in pointless meetings or writing reports that never serve any real purpose?

In many senses it's about what I call self-honesty. We have a great capacity for misleading ourselves. This is often so subtle that we believe our own deception. We procrastinate, delay or reach hypothetical conclusions that prevent us taking action. Without doubt, one of our greatest hurdles is self-doubt. That in-built fear that most of us seem to keep in reserve for difficult and challenging moments. What might have been originally designed to protect us now regularly holds us back.

Not everything we're going to do will hit the right spot. Inevitably, there are necessary tasks that we don't look forward to. But instead of putting them off, it's much better to deal with them as quickly and efficiently as possible and move on to something better. Not leave them lying around taking up valuable headspace while we worry about not doing them.

We all know people who seem to crack through work at a pace that leaves others in their wake. Are they so much brighter or working longer hours? Usually not. They're the sort of people who have their own version of *The Monday Revolution* and apply it within the rules and culture of their organisation. In short, they've worked out how to get things done.

Over the coming chapters, we'll explore everyday tasks and topics you can apply to revolutionise your approach to work. I'll be covering all those challenging areas that just seem to get in the way, providing real hands-on practical advice that I apply in my own Monday Revolution.

The Monday Revolution will transform how you think about the things that really matter and help you achieve your goals in a highly time-efficient way. You'll find a summary at the end of each section, which will provide a quick reference to help solve those important daily issues.

Chapter 1
Who's in charge around here?
Good leader, bad leader

We can all recall bosses we feared, respected or loathed. Some had a major impact on our lives, often extending beyond the workplace. True examples of the best and worst of management behaviour. No doubt we said to ourselves that should our lucky day come, we would remember these times and do our best to manage others as we would like to have been treated ourselves.

Having progressed from the shop floor in a factory making light bulbs to chief executive and director of many companies, I've made more than my fair share of slip-ups along the way. I can recall with horror some of the things I did, which at the time I thought were best practice.

For example, I went through a phase of telling candidates at the end of an interview they hadn't got the job. And then I'd tell them why. Unsurprisingly, this led to anger and in some cases tears. To me it seemed expedient, but I think most people would have preferred a softer, written response to immediate outright rejection.

Many, many years later I still meet people I've long forgotten who can still recall an interview with me. Not necessarily because they were brutally rejected after 30 minutes but because the direct questions and challenges were unexpected. For some, this was a good experience and others found it intimidating. At that time, I probably only employed the more confident candidates and a cleverer, more thoughtful technique would have resulted in a more diverse workforce. Assembling the right evidence to support my decision would have helped no end. I realise that now.

I hope I learnt from my mistakes and over many years improved. And that when I became a leader of a large organisation, I hadn't completely forgotten what it's like to be on the front line and not been seduced by the so called 'C Suite'. Never perfect, but I think I always recognised where the front line was and would readily join it myself when the situation required it.

I say this because I often find organisations where the managers and the front line seem to have a kind of 'no man's land' between them. But here's an example where the opposite is true.

This company has, over many years, created a bond between the leadership team and the people who do the practical work. In this instance, the front line is made up of highly skilled people, experts in serious illness and community care.

This is a business that operates 24/7 in a very tough environment. It's in a sector where money and resources are tight. It needs a cohesive, pull-together approach with strong leadership. The leader and her senior team have created a really strong model of great working practice that's really worth sharing.

Managers can go missing from the front line, leaving others to fight fires and deal with the problems as best they can. But not in this company. The organisation and its people operate in such a way that their real potential and resourcefulness is allowed to show itself. This has, I'm sure to a great extent, become learned behaviour from the team leader. People really do follow the example of those in charge. If they engage with their teams, are notable because they are often seen and promote the challenges of their people in a positive upward manner, it gets spotted. And, would you believe it? Often their behaviour is replicated down the line.

The company has a board of directors and an experienced chairman. They need to be on side too. Being a leader isn't easy. There are plenty of people on the board that need to keep believing in you. This might be true of your situation. Or perhaps your company is just starting out, and hiring others to provide oversight and experience is yet to reach your to do-list. Never mind.

Monday Revolutions come in a variety of forms, shapes and sizes. What matters is the championing of your people. The consequences of not engaging with the front line are high sickness rates, staff turnover and low morale. A tragedy, really, which could be easily put right.

The lesson here is crystal clear. If you want to get the best from your organisation, make sure you spend time with the people who the organisation depends on for success. And you can't do this in a token way. You're not on a state visit. You should participate in meetings, meet customers, buy the beers in the pub, say a few words at anniversaries, birthdays and even leaving drinks. Sometimes it feels awkward, but it has to be done. There is only one way to lead and that's from the front. Knowing when to be highly visible, when it really matters, is a demonstration of true leadership. Going missing when the chips are down is a dereliction of duty.

During my time at Capital Radio we bought many other radio companies. In some instances, we were welcomed as the new owner. They saw increased opportunity in being part of a larger organisation, but that wasn't always the case. I remember visiting our latest "purchase" to say hello and answer any questions. I stood there in front of a large group of people who made it very clear they weren't very pleased to see me. Nobody asked any questions and eventually the local guy in charge said there had been a lot of historic ownership problems. They were proud people and had no wish to be owned by a London-based company that was very likely to destroy their local identity – as had happened in the past.

The local manager said he'd been given some anonymous questions to ask me. The first of which was why could people earn more in McDonald's flipping burgers? You get the drift.

I wasn't expecting this to be honest. Maybe treating them as a "purchase" in all but name had come across to them prior to my visit. Just using that one word among my colleagues had been interpreted by them and sent some early negative messages. I agreed to visit the business in the future and get involved in activities, providing they were useful, and also have some fun. It took a while to gain their trust, but over time it worked out for all of us.

Be visible, starting next Monday. A small effort here will transform your standing and your business. Don't be the kind of manager who only appears when mistakes are made. Celebrating the success of others is part of good practice, not a sign of weakness.

The Monday Revolution (you can start on Monday)

1. Leadership is about recognising when to be visible. You can't lead an organisation unless people know who you are and what you stand for.

2. Spend time with the front line. Get to know individuals and how they spend their day. Your direct reports may protest that this is undermining them. Make sure it isn't, but don't let that possibility stop you doing it.

3. Make a commitment to being a visible, in-touch leader, by building a plan into your working week. Being too busy and not making the effort to stay in touch simply isn't good enough. But don't steal the limelight or all the glory either!

Chapter 2
The Horse's Mouth
Communication from you

As a species we're told that we're highly sociable creatures and enjoy communicating. Isolation and loneliness are very definitely to be avoided, if possible, at all costs. We have the tools to get this right: a common language and culture. Communication rules aren't written down, but from an early age we know roughly what they are.

Like many things in life and business, it's not that straight-forward. My idea of good communication may not be yours. But wherever you are on this, liking more information or less, I've never heard anyone complain that their company or boss over-communicates. "They just tell us too much, constantly."

This part of *The Monday Revolution* is an attempt to let you know just a couple of things really. Confirmation that some of what you do is on the right track, and the possibility that there are some ideas you don't practise that might help if you did. To win *The Monday Revolution* you have to get your message across, or nothing will ever change.

I've worked with people whose idea of communication was simply telling. By that, I mean there was no interaction or dialogue. More like a statement you might hear a lawyer read on their behalf on the steps of a courthouse. Such occasions rarely resonate and inevitably provoke questions that remain unanswered.

In the workplace, and elsewhere, communication seems to have become a struggle in some respects. Companies wrestle with what to say and how and when to say it. Is no communication better than poor or misleading words? Is it better to deny redundancies will happen with a fudge until they do? Or say up front they're a possibility, and scare everyone, most of whom will not be leaving? Do you embrace best practice with a senior management consultation process only to obfuscate the answer and leave the team wondering what will happen next? Something? Anything? Nothing?

At Capital Radio, my predecessor had a good reputation for communicating. Luckily, I could learn from him. I enjoyed the challenge of getting the message across and being questioned on what I'd just said. Many people don't share my enthusiasm and often, unfortunately, increased seniority results in self-inflicted isolation and distance from the people they should be close to.

As my career developed, I adopted the opposite stance to withdrawal and isolation. It's interesting because until my twenties I was hopelessly shy. Yet as time went on, I grew in confidence and I relished letting everyone know what was going on and why. If in doubt, I said more not less. I tried to avoid surprising people by paving the way for what might be on the horizon:

"OK everyone, it's approaching budget time and sales have been difficult, we're going to be prudent and assume that will continue. We need to be responsibly cautious. We're doing everything we can to build the business, but we can't assume the market will change.

So please don't factor in more people or increased costs because we'll not be doing that this year. Those exciting new projects will have to wait I'm afraid."

That was part of a regular update I gave all 300 people at our headquarters in London. In addition to me, many others would speak giving brief updates and we all took questions.

The problem I had was the other 1,500 people who worked in the company weren't in the building. They were spread across the UK from the West Country to central Scotland. So, I decided to do two things. I scheduled regular visits to each of our other locations, as did my colleagues. But to ensure current information reached everyone quickly, more or less at that same time, we created The Horse's Mouth.

I was the Horse and if you heard it from me, you could assume it was important, true and happening. I did this by conference call with the management at each of our locations, sometimes in groups. Prior to speaking, they had each asked their teams for questions for me to respond to. Which I did. We noted all the calls so we could make sure we addressed common themes and could respond with more specific answers when needed.

In addition, we used email and the occasional video to support our communication efforts. But anything of significance was always face to face or the closest we could get to that. We built a culture which supported not saving things up. I wanted to avoid being a place where all the news was stored and delivered in an untimely way.

I remembered in my days as an engineering draughtsman being on the end of a critical probationary review. If only I'd been told, as a new person, what I was failing at, I could have corrected it. But no one let me know and I was fired.

My personal approach is much more transparent and straightforward. I always let people I work with know where they stand. Appraisals and reviews contain no shocks or revelations. Too many times people approach these badly conducted affairs with a great deal of trepidation. Why? Because until that meeting, they really didn't know how they're viewed and valued. No real communication at all. "I thought I might get fired but they said nice things and gave me a pay rise." Oh dear. What a very sad way to run a company.

If you're the type of leader who could easily die at the thought of standing in front of your people, you need to get help. Because it's not optional. Being senior is about many things. And in your case, communication and leadership are inseparable. I always used to say anyone can give good news, but I've even seen that go wrong. If you recognise help is needed, there's plenty out there and it really is possible to make significant improvement. Find an expert to develop your skills (you have them) and build your confidence.

As a child and teenager, I was the goofy ginger-headed kid with little confidence. When it came to reading in class out loud I hated it. School plays and assembly were strictly no-go areas; I went off sick. Somehow, I managed to circumnavigate this problem until my career necessitated presenting information to others in a formal setting. The only thing I could do was write a script and read it without looking up. But what soon followed was the requirement to face an audience with charts and free-form speech. Insomnia took over for the weeks and days beforehand.

But luckily, help showed up when my boss suggested we both went on a two-day course. Our trainer was exceptional and gave me the confidence to present, ad-lib, handle questions and get my key points across. It took many years to perfect and I'm still a "work in progress". But I've gone from total avoidance to seeking out opportunities to communicate. When I don't do it, I miss it. An extraordinary turnaround. Proof that in spite of what we believe about our own capabilities, in the right hands, others can see potential that we fail to spot.

As a leader, communication isn't optional. People need regular information and if you're at the helm of a public company the calendar of these events is published as a matter of record. If you're stewarding someone else's money, then a whole set of rules are in place to ensure you do the right thing. Anything that might influence the share price needs to be announced when it's known. Otherwise the shares are trading in what's known as a false market. And that's not on. As my chairman used to say, "get this wrong and you'll end up in prison. And you won't want to share a cell with me". He was right!

Listed companies, almost without exception, retain the service of a specialist communication company to help manage the messages and logistics. Often these work in tandem with the chief executive's in-house team in order to get all the ducks lined up. For me this worked pretty well. We had a good team all round and we kept it simple on announcement days. Clear messages backed up with supporting evidence and a well-rehearsed question and answer plan.

A tip I've used many times is to always write a concise, one-page, press release. Not because it would be released, necessarily, but to provide clarity and focus. The thinking goes that if you can't write the rational explanation of whatever it is on a one-page release and make sense, then what you're about to do is probably a bad idea.

My reputation, I'm told, is one of a good communicator. Clear, brief, timely, honest and prepared to be questioned. To provide balance I'm also described as blunt, heavy-handed and sometimes insensitive. In that the message is fine but the packaging could be better. I'm working on that.

I've worked with many impressive people, like my friend and previous boss at Capital, Richard Eyre. I often wish that I had his eloquence and turn of phrase. In presenting a critical appraisal to a colleague he'd say: "I'd like to help you avoid the mistakes I've made." That type of sentence would have been unlikely to have found its way out of my mouth, sadly.

Being the type of leader who's visible and accessible is generally a good thing, I believe. We've all worked with or know people who couldn't tell you what the management look like, or what they do all day. I made a point of telling people about my week. But it can occasionally put you in a difficult position when you least expect it.

I was invited to celebrate a birthday at an after-hours office drinks party by the guys who ran one of our radio stations a couple of floors away. I enjoyed these moments so was very happy to show up, recognising a few short words might be needed. On that occasion they weren't, but the team were very keen for me to meet a guy who unfortunately I didn't recognise. Thinking he was a new team member, I asked him if he was a programme or a sales colleague. To which he replied in an American accent that he was neither. The small crowd around us were amused, shocked and embarrassed, all at the same time.

"I'm Kanye West," he volunteered. "Of course you are, let me find you some more champagne."

I'm a regular speaker for a charity called Speakers for Schools. They ask you to speak at state schools, anything from assembly to a small class. I always tell that story. It never fails to grab the attention of teenagers and provides me with some reverse credibility. Yes, I mix with the stars but I've no idea who they are.

But don't let the odd bad gig put you off. Communication is so important that it shouldn't be treated casually or as something discretionary. No one expects you to be Winston Churchill or the Queen's toastmaster. But the art and science of communication are the keys to unlocking so many doors that will otherwise remain closed.

The Monday Revolution (you can start on Monday)

1. Acknowledge leadership and communication are inseparable.
2. Never assume people know what's going on so there's no real need to explain. They don't, and by saying so you're using that as a reason for not standing up and doing the right thing.
3. Agree with your team what regular communication should look like. Draw up a plan, tell people what to expect and deliver it. It really isn't that hard.
4. Recognise that in tough times communication needs to be stepped up – regardless of whether it's to your

people or those outside. Do not disappear when people expect to see you.

5. Enjoy the experience. Being known for good communication is a great accolade and can really set you apart from others who choose to avoid this important leadership responsibility and skill.

Chapter 3
Join us, there's a Pret next door
Hiring

"We find it really hard to employ good people." Well, how many times have you heard that, or probably said it yourself? Even worse, you think you've hired the right person only to find they don't work out.

The Industrial Revolution is a long way behind us and the UK is now, primarily, a service-based economy. Substituting a manufacturing industry for people-based companies has made the recruitment of smart people a top priority for most organisations.

The good news is, without too much effort, there's a lot more companies can do to make better hiring decisions. Reviewing existing processes can really pay dividends, if improvements are properly applied. And it's not just about recruiting the right people; it's ensuring they stay motivated and grow with the business. Thankfully, hire and fire has been consigned to history for the most part. Fairness, diversity and equality are much better watch words.

Applying your approach to employment consistently has the benefit of ensuring you, and those around you, don't need to reinvent what should be a developed and successful process.

Much has changed for the better in society and your complementary, diversified workforce should reflect this evolving state of affairs. But it's unlikely to happen on its own; you'll need to have the right principles in place.

So how might a company go about improving their chances of employing good people? There's so much most companies can do to shorten the odds in their favour. It's a case of reviewing the whole process and confirming the methods chosen are the correct ones to identify and review the right candidate.

It sounds obvious, but as a starting point, ensure your public face is making the right impression. If your public presence isn't up to scratch, it will cost you quality candidates. Who wants to join a business that hasn't taken the trouble to present itself in the right way? This has little to do with the expense, much more to do with awareness. So many people complain about their own companies' online presence: "I'm sorry, our website is pretty crap; we're supposed to be updating it."

One of my regular seminars for business leaders is centred around building high-performing teams. To succeed at this, you've got to hire the right people in the first place. At my event, I've looked at the public image of all the companies present, usually around 20, on the basis that top talent is going to be sought after and more likely to want to work for a company that, at least at a superficial level, looks attractive.

When I start to explain what I've done, the people in the room tend to look embarrassed and worry that I'll single out their company for a shabby look. I don't. I just highlight two or three that present an attractive dynamic image. On one memorable occasion it included an engineering company from Birmingham and a biotech from Cambridge. Both were delighted and really pleased that their efforts to portray a great image had been recognised.

When I joined Capital Radio as commercial director, I had a disappointing early experience. On air the company was always irritatingly optimistic and upbeat. Yet their physical reception area was a dingy mess of poor-quality merchandise and people sheltering from the rain. I still joined but I did get it changed. I remember saying to Richard, the then chief executive, had he noticed the disappointment on the faces of listeners and advertising customers as they entered the building? They were expecting a welcome that represented the on-air persona. When we relocated to Leicester Square, in the centre of London, we made amends and it was no longer an issue.

After image, the second priority is being clear about what you want the person to do. Not just now, but in the future as well. If they're going to progress and will need additional skills at a senior level, identify those required attributes at the recruitment stage. Too many times I've worked with companies who've promoted an executive to a senior position and expected them to have skills they've never even possessed. Or skills they've never been able to easily develop and worryingly probably never will.

I'm sorry, but some accountants, engineers and IT people are never going to be killer sales or commercial people. And certainly vice versa! Yet, when promoted to partner or director, that's often what's expected. Disappointment, stress and anxiety inevitably follow.

Job descriptions often fall way short of what's required. They are often a revamp of something drawn up some time ago, or more likely the work of someone in "the people department", abundant with platitudes and corporate speak. It really is very important to be precise about the skills and experience that match the job requirement.

Companies struggle to find "really good" people because they don't spend anywhere near enough time considering what they really need. Knowing the right person when you see them is not a successful strategy.

The next stage is as critical as the first two and is often where hiring mistakes are frequently made. If you were buying a company you wouldn't take their word for the fact they say they are a great business, would you? Of course not. You'd do a considerable amount of due diligence digging, to ensure you weren't being sold a pup. But when hiring people there is a great propensity to rely on personal judgement and gut feel. Important of course, but only if supported by evidence. And gathering facts about people can be tough, but not impossible.

When interviewing, I have a set of questions directly related to how I will judge that person's performance. I provide examples of situations I know will confront them and ask how they will respond. I ask the candidate to provide me with examples of how they have managed similar encounters. I require them to provide evidence to support their answers.

The important point is the emphasis is on them to provide the evidence, not for you to seek it out (although, of course, you'll be doing your own due diligence). To supplement this, add to the process some exercises very specific to the position. If the job requires them to write board papers, make them write one for you.

Take references, if not the current employer then the previous ones. It's increasingly difficult these days, as people are frightened of being sued, but some will be helpful if not bound by a corporate policy of silence.

And take professional outside help to provide independent assessment. Personally, I favour psychometric testing to reveal traits such as energy levels, problem solving and other important areas not always apparent at interview.

I recently discussed this approach with a company that has a poor record of attracting the right people and then keeping them. Until now, the company took the view that you can't question and challenge senior candidates because they're above it and would be offended. They're not the only company I know to take this approach.

They each interview the candidate, have dinner or lunch a couple of times and then make the hire. Unsurprisingly, it's not particularly successful. I've been hired myself as a non-executive board member in exactly that fashion. There's an assumption that because I'm a successful director in one business, I'm the right person to sit at their board table. Of course, I shared the responsibility to ensure it made sense from my side as well. I have to say that in more than one instance, it didn't go well for either of us.

But back to the central point: avoiding the pitfalls and improving the chances of making a great hiring. A common situation that regularly occurs is that of senior people applying for a role in a much smaller business. There's appeal in the big fish, small pond syndrome and I get that. Lost and overlooked in a large sprawling organisation, there's much to be said for working in a much smaller company. Often it goes like this:

> "We've some good news, a very senior guy from Google has applied for our CRO (Chief Revenue Officer) role.

I wouldn't have expected someone like that to be interested. But I've had a meeting with him and he's really keen. Wants to work in a much smaller coalface environment and has a really great network of contacts."

This could be a significant hiring for the company. Being the sort of small organisation that can attract talent from global corporations, who presumably have many career choices, is very flattering. And it's great to tell shareholders and investors (if you have them) that the company is recognised as a go-to place.

These candidates tell us what we like to hear. And they're certainly being genuine about it. Big companies that have lost their way. Laden with corporate rules that stifle innovation. Imported in-house regulations from elsewhere don't help and therefore the time has come for them to apply their talents in the world of fast and nimble.

I have seen this work really well in some companies and disastrously in others. There is no doubt that acquiring big-name talent can make a very positive impact. Not just very senior people, but those who have also been expensively trained in a big corporate environment and are looking to move to somewhere less constraining.

To illustrate this point here's an example of how it can easily trap you into believing what you want to hear. Some time ago, I joined a newish company as chairman in waiting. The business was a tech company specialising in state-of-the-art video production and had attracted a lot of outside investment. As part of my induction, the chief executive asked me to meet various team members. The creative IT guy fitted the stereotype. Hoodie, limited eye contact and a vocabulary that supposed I had a detailed knowledge of coding. If only. Nevertheless, we enjoyed our time together building virtual worlds on screen and discussing the commercial application and appeal for customers.

Next up was the CRO proudly recruited from a global tech business where he'd spent the last ten years or so. He was a very charming, friendly guy who was delightful to spend time with. He explained how he'd recruited the team into this very small company from other big-name players, and that it was a very important endorsement of the company plan that these people had joined. So far, so good. Of course, this talented team didn't join for peanuts, so to cover their own costs at least they needed to run pretty fast.

We looked at revenue generated against the business plan. The gap was significant. We discussed the challenges around that and what initiatives were in place to create sales. What became apparent was that these commercial hires from big-name companies had zero experience in taking a sales proposition to a new market. Their contacts were the wrong people, so in effect they brought no existing relationships into the company when they joined.

Furthermore, their former experience was all reactive. By that I mean incoming briefs were handed out and their role was to respond with a proposal that fitted the request. Tramping the streets of London making multiple meetings with new contacts just wasn't on their radar.

"How many sales have you made?" I asked the CRO. "That's not my job," he replied. "I manage the team." Said it all really. They all left and so did I. The chief executive likened my participation to having his homework marked. He didn't respond well to accountability. I wished him luck.

But I also work with companies where the outcome has been far more positive. With people who are much less comfortable in a rules-based environment. Or those who feel they've been unfairly passed over in the promotion stakes and acknowledge their future is probably best organised elsewhere. Often these types flourish; I've seen this on many occasions. Interestingly, they often recommend previous colleagues to join them. A great endorsement for the company they work for now.

It's important to understand the motivations in both instances. You can sometimes hire big names that will succeed in a smaller company environment. These people are able to adapt to a more hands-on accountable way of life. They don't need the back-up and resources of a large corporation. Equally, highly trained professionals from global corporations can have spent years hiding in what can be a too-forgiving organisation. When they are eventually moved on, it can be the smaller companies that take up the slack.

"Hey, we've just made a great hire from Kellogg." Only to find that Kellogg finally bit the underperformance bullet and their problem child has just been adopted by you.

The Monday Revolution (you can start on Monday)

1. First impressions are important. Make sure your image is the best it can be.
2. Describe the role in a clear, positive and dynamic way. If it reads like a job written by somebody who doesn't understand what they're doing, you'll not be making a great hire.

3. Take personal responsibility for the first two points.
4. Ask candidates to provide evidence to support their claims. If they can't, don't hire them. And do your own digging.
5. Have a proven process for employing people. Use tests, psychologists, practical exercises. Good people won't mind. In fact, they'll be impressed with your diligence.
6. Hiring people is a gamble. Shorten the odds to get the best result you can. And remember, once they've arrived chucking them in the deep end until some meaningless probationary meeting isn't the best approach.

Chapter 4
Sticks and carrots
Pay and reward

Not long into my eight-year tenure as CEO of Capital Radio, I was confronted with an important decision. Chris Tarrant was our number one DJ and his London Breakfast Show generated millions in advertising and sponsorship revenue. He had a fixed-term contract with some time to run. Anticipating the negotiation, his agent secured a written offer from one of our closest competitors, Heart FM, to double his pay to one million pounds a year if he joined them and left us.

To be honest, with everything else going on I could have really done without this. Furthermore, his publicist was turning up the heat by feeding the Daily Mail stories that he was unhappy with the early starts and fancied a change. The company share price reacted and I needed to solve the problem.

I needed to bite the bullet but which one?

Promote another DJ? Search the market for a replacement? Or do a deal with Chris? As you'd expect, we considered these options carefully. I discussed the situation with our board of directors at our next meeting.

One director said: "Paying the first million-pound salary is always the hardest." He worked at a bank where I assumed this was just pocket money.

That seem to swing the mood in the favour of Chris remaining, which quite frankly was my favoured option. After much toing and froing, we reached agreement. Fortunate, as I didn't really have a plan B we were confident in. And searching the market is always tricky. Although much later on that's what we ended up doing.

Eventually we agreed new terms with Chris and his agent that kept him out of the arms of an aggressive competitor. The thought of him broadcasting for them and taking his loyal audience with him was keeping me awake at night.

I resolved to build a good relationship with Chris, not just rely on his agent, and groom a successor. Lessons learnt and I didn't want to get caught again.

The truth is, I should have known better. Identifying your key executives, building relationships with them and ensuring the temptation to move elsewhere is not on their radar is pretty fundamental.

As a business leader this is a top priority. If you don't have high-flying people around you building products, running operations or whatever your business requires, you'll run into trouble sooner or later.

There are many things you can do to ensure a motivated workforce but one of the most difficult to get right is the tricky issue of pay and reward. In theory, it should be a relatively simple exercise. The business world is awash with experienced managers, consultants and other experts ready to help.

There are many precedents for every industry, yet what we pay and reward people seems to be as contentious as ever. Out of all the questions I get from businesses, "How should we reward our people?" is among the most frequent.

"The thing is, I don't want to sound ungrateful, but I think I deserve more."

"I could earn more elsewhere, what I'm paid is way below my market rate."

"Others at my level are paid more than me."

"New people are earning more than we do", and many more phrases you'll be very familiar with, no doubt.

"On reflection, I think I'm overpaid. Please reduce my salary" – yet to hear this one.

If you're the boss, stuck in the middle between your superior (perhaps in title only) and the front-line troops, all this is the kind of pain you can do without. You don't want to lose good people but you've a budget to recognise and often it's the same people putting you under pressure. The high-flyers, confident their direct approach won't be saved up and retaliated against at some point, feel they're acting from a strong position.

Like everything else it's a people problem where blanket policies and company doctrine are great in theory, but increasingly irrelevant to the individual and the everyday working world. At one time, an annual blanket pay rise was commonplace, everyone received the same and the only way of beating the system was to be promoted. In theory, it has great merit of course. Nothing to really think about. Everyone knows the rules, no one steps out of line and the company can accurately predict its labour cost. Link the rise to inflation and the whole idea can be easily justified.

I recall working at a company where there was a proud defence of the rigid pay and reward system. But what do you do when this happens?

"The thing is David, everyone here understands the system. An inflation linked rise for all and company profit share on top at the end of the year."

A simple system easily communicated, no argument with that.

So far, so good. Until the high-flyers from the IT development division discovered the market valued them more than their current bosses. Slowly and surely the exodus began, as the grass on the other side really was much greener. Ever in denial, the CEO, having blamed managers, HR and unscrupulous head-hunters, had to face up to the fact that his policy to motivate and retain his key people needed a radical rethink.

Not least because the cost of replacement was significant. New candidates were far more expensive than the leavers. They were on long notice periods and were not prepared to join a pay and reward system that ignored market value and personal performance.

What did the company do? Well, it first had to recognise the problem and acknowledge there was an issue. This was difficult and involved all sorts of discussions, which inevitably became wide ranging in their scope. Everything from company culture to extra benefits. All important elements that we'll return to, but the truth is unless you get to the central issue, adding free beer and a staff discount isn't going to cut it.

New candidates of quality are usually confidently aware of their negotiating position.

"Look, this is a really important decision for me. The job seems perfect and I know I'll make a great contribution. From what I've seen it's a brilliant culture and the possibilities to advance are really going to motivate me. But the basic package is less than I currently earn and to be honest I'm looking for a step up. I've had many approaches with more money, which I've said no to because the position wasn't quite right. This is the job I'd love but I need another 20% on what you're offering."

So say many candidates in a variety of different ways. Of course, they wanted at least market rate or above and that meant the company's fixed-tiered system would be broken, providing that a different set of pay rules, just for new people, could be put in place. Or the company could employ lesser people for less money, hardly a good idea if you're trying to grow a business, which I assume you are.

Government-sponsored organisations are typical of rigid, inflexible thinking on pay and reward. Levels, tiers and bands are commonly used to fix remuneration, inevitably geared to treasury budgets. These provide the foundation for an increasingly dissatisfied workforce until only the committed, desperate and challenged candidates take the jobs. Then there'll be public outcry about the quality of teachers, the lack of nurses and the politicians will blame the previous regime and put in place a catch-up pay plan and recruitment drive. Then the whole sorry, sad cycle will start again to be repeated a few years down the line.

It's so short-term and damaging. Recruiting people into many industries takes years. You can't train a doctor on a three-month course at the local Travelodge. If you make entire sectors unattractive, the recovery period stretches out over the years.

Crazy. As we know to our cost, those that ignore history tend to repeat it, as the saying goes.

Another example of an extreme system, which I also don't advocate, is that normally attributed to bankers. The annual bonus. This method of reward is prevalent in many, many industries outside of finance. It's just that bankers, for a number of very well-trodden reasons, are singled out to take the media hit.

Mostly, annual bonuses appear to be part of an opaque system that has little apparent relationship to performance or productivity. That's why they're seen as a problem. Existing only because everybody else has them, so as to be competitive. "We need them too. It doesn't mean we like them!" Where's the courage in that?

In the world of work, everyone has their calling. And those arguments of why nurses (I'm married to one) are at the bottom of the pay scale, taking account of the demands of an absolutely necessary service, compared to bankers, are largely mean-ingless. Bankers become bankers because they want to make money. Nurses are nurses for very different reasons. And to be fair, if we don't create wealth and generate taxes, we wouldn't be able to pay anyone in free health care. What they both share are pay and reward systems that are not fit for purpose and we, outside of these extremes, can learn and apply more successful strategies and models.

As business people we remain, mostly, only tied to the norms of the market and the expectations of our people, present and future. Within the financial constraints of our company, we enjoy complete discretion on how we decide to pay those around us.

Everything should be at our disposal, and an open-minded approach can benefit everyone involved. On the one hand, we have the ability to pay according to hours worked and can employ a flexible workforce according to demand. Only paying staff when you need them is a useful variable cost, geared to the direct immediate needs of the business.

This needs careful thought and management, as the downside for the worker is they never know what they'll earn that week – not helpful for planning outgoings and paying the bills. Being fair and responsible with this style of reward is about ensuring a good reputation, which will help attract talented people. You don't want to be the employer of last resort.

"I'm only working here until I can find something else. For what they pay I'm almost better off on benefits." People saying things like this at the bottom end of the pay scale will have an impact all the way to the top and probably into the media. Not what you want, as that will affect recruitment and morale at all levels.

At the other end of the scale, the average pay package of a FTSE or Fortune 100 chief executive runs into millions. And it appears that all too often there is only a tenuous link to performance. Profits and share price slide in the wrong direction, but salaries in the senior executive suite have been growing for largely inexplicable reasons.

The worst case is exploited workers at one end and the clichéd fat cats at the other. Millions of words have been written on the subject and it's not my intention to add further to the volumes of criticism. But I would like to look at a few common issues and offer some advice, which in my experience has every chance of working. It works for me and the companies I'm involved in.

First, be honest about what sort of company you're running. Are you the type of company where people say, "trouble is, they don't pay very well"? If attracting great people is part of your plan, then that's a reputation you can do without. If you're a company that's known for paying well *and* respecting your colleagues, in my view that's attractive. Particularly in a competitive recruitment market.

Base salary is the driver for other benefits, the most important of which is a pension (if you provide one), followed by incentive schemes and performance-related pay. If you don't keep up with market rates, you fall into the trap of paying new hires at better rates than your loyal incumbents. Who, if you're not careful, will soon work out that the only way to get a pay rise is to leave. Recognising that good people are hard to find, don't lose the ones you have already.

Avoid blanket pay rises because you'll inevitably be rewarding people as if they all perform at the same level of productivity. And they most certainly don't. Use the under-performers' allocation to hit above the market benchmark for the key achievers. In virtually every company, pay increases are discretionary. Yet too often someone on the wrong end of a difficult appraisal still benefits from the company increase. It is remarkable how often someone in the firing line for underperformance still gets paid more.

> "Why do you think I should leave? You just gave me a pay rise!"

The much trickier areas to get right are bonuses, incentives and discretionary rewards. If you're not careful, these can be counterproductive and, in the worst instances, divisive. On the other hand, performance-related pay (PRP) can improve productivity. Some time ago I was a director of a business where we scrapped annual discretionary bonuses for PRP. It made a really important, positive difference.

With discretionary bonuses, no one really knew what they had to do to get paid out. At the end of the year (far too long) they'd be given their number, which mostly disappointed. Their expectations hadn't been managed and had got out of hand. Furthermore, they suspected that others had done better than them. My experience has taught me these pooled bonus schemes are mostly useless and not fit for purpose.

I worked at a company which was mostly owned by the founder. The remuneration meeting decisions were mostly based on their personal experience of meeting staff in the company restaurant.

CEO: "What are you saying we should pay Laura next year and what bonus this year?"

HR director: "Well, her director has recommended a 10% salary uplift and a 30% bonus."

CEO: "Yes, I'm happy with that, pleasant lady, had a good chat with her last week about sailing – didn't realise she sailed."

HR director: "He's recommending the same for John."

CEO: "No. Absolutely not. Doesn't clear his plates away at lunchtime. He's worth half that."

It may seem unreal, but I've witnessed, many times, these subjective prejudiced approaches to pay and reward. And promotions too. Where available evidence is downgraded or cast aside for an emotional, subjective view. This is not *The Monday Revolution* way of carrying on.

At a very different company, one of our managers was absolutely clear that reward equated to performance, not their ability to talk a good game. "We're deciding whether they've performed, not whether we want to go on holiday with them."

For me, annual bonuses and discretionary rewards have no place in the companies I'm involved in. In some instances, I'm still trying to win that battle, as in many places these things are ingrained and not easily removed. But the logic for doing something better is compelling and the arguments for preserving the status quo increasingly weak.

Talk to an interview candidate about a generous discretionary bonus scheme and they'll mostly value it at zero. A nice-to-have maybe, but who knows where the hurdles will be set and anyway doesn't discretionary mean just that?

Work is a financial and emotional contract between a company and a person. Do these things and we'll pay you what we agreed. Do more than those things, go the extra mile, and we'll pay you more. We expect you to uphold the values of the company in the course of doing your work, which includes appropriate behaviour and getting on with your colleagues.

Of course, it's possible to closely define all of these things and create an endless list of objectives, which would rather defeat the purpose of this book. So, we'll not do that.

By applying some basic principles it's entirely possible to have a motivated individual and team. Just make sure you're clear about what you want people to do, agree that with them, and pay them for it. Too often, reward discussions are an annual event, geared to a review or appraisal. Never a good idea, as the 12-month gap is far too long to achieve anything remotely useful.

Here's what I mean:

Manager: "We're five months into the year and running 30% behind budget; it's not looking great is it?"

Executive: "Yes. Obviously, we're aware of that but the sales pipeline is really strong for the last quarter and we're confident of pulling it back."

In my experience that never happens. If the company, its target and individual PRP had been geared to shorter, sharper timeframes, a different result might have been achieved. Why? Because it would have been in their personal interest to deal with the problem earlier, that's why.

The 12-month lead time to final achievement suits the finance director for budgeting reasons. But for the executive it's too far away to be meaningful. Time slips away, the orders don't come in and before you know it targets are becoming increasingly tougher to hit in an ever-decreasing window of opportunity. Everything backs up.

Much better to incentivise people or small teams on a quarterly basis, against a measurable set of objectives. The key questions are – how do we want these people to behave? What exactly do we need them to do over the coming weeks? Smart companies know this and do it. Lesser organisations, some of which I've been involved in, deceive themselves into thinking it will all come good in the second half. Then the last quarter. Then it doesn't.

Agree the measures of success and reward according to performance and results. Everybody knows where they stand and there are no unpleasant shocks or surprises. Importantly, the money you're paying out is for increased productivity. Not a post-Christmas gift which mostly disappoints.

A chief executive I work with and I devised a scheme some time ago which works pretty well, that you might want to try. We agree the tasks and priorities for the year. Everything from beating budget to promoting the company by speaking at a couple of conferences. And around ten things in between. "For 100% achievement, he can earn an additional 50% of annual salary." The clever bit is we weight each task according to priority, so beating budget earns more than getting on stage. Following each quarter, we review progress and at the end of the year we add up the weighted average, congratulate and pay out.

This method resulted in a chief executive who agreed his priorities, reviewed them regularly with his boss and was paid for performance. It's not rocket science, yet many companies struggle with the concept.

I remember one chairman saying, "Great idea in theory David, but it has a major flaw in it. It assumes we know what they're supposed to be doing in the first place!"

To attract the right talent, earn a reputation for competitive pay and reward. Incentivise people to perform through simple transparent schemes. And above all, be seen to treat people fairly.

The Monday Revolution (you can start on Monday)

1. Establish market demand and reward for all your key people. Review their contracts. Keep ahead or you'll lose them.

2. When hiring, make your advertisement, invitation, head-hunter call or whatever more appealing than everyone else's. This will not be hard.

3. Promote what you do inside and outside the organisation. Be one of those companies you've heard of but rarely worked for: "No point in approaching her, too well looked after."

4. Design a salary-based performance-related pay scheme for everybody. Yes, everybody. And if you don't know what they do or why they're here, make a saving.

5. Measure everything in quarterly time segments across the year. You can roll them up, combine them or whatever else but anything longer and you'll never create momentum. Just imagine you operate three-month years if that helps.

6. Ensure appraisals and rewards are aligned. You're paying for behaviour in all its forms. Don't appraise people for one thing and pay them for doing something else.

Chapter 5
Who's made the cut?
Building high-performance teams

The appetite for knowing how to build a winning team shows no sign of abating. And why would it? Winning teams, well, they win, don't they? And whatever business you're in, winning takes precedence.

It's interesting in that I was raised on a different notion – "it's not about the winning, it's about the taking part". In my early years that was, apparently, more than just all right. In fact, demonstrations of ambition and success, well, they just weren't socially acceptable. Then in my adult years this unambitious mediocrity was savagely replaced by a personal world of accountability. Where winning orders, new customers or the sales prize was the only thing that counted. Failure equalled dismissal.

The Monday Revolution approach to attracting high performers requires an all-round approach. As detailed in the previous chapter, the company's outward presentation needs to be compelling. Dull, out-dated marketing materials and a tired old website isn't going to make the shortlist, as far as the candidate is concerned. And there's little point in those factors working well if the job description falls short of dynamic, having been written by a trainee in the people department. Or some similar often unconnected outpost. You need to ensure your company looks like (and pays like) a business going somewhere. High performers want high-performance environments. It's where they can raise their game and flourish.

Like so much in business there's demand for a formula requirement that will solve the problem. And to some extent they exist. Identifying how companies have built winning teams and copying their behaviour can provide some answers. But too often organisations think it can be achieved quickly by adopting certain elements, but not the whole ingredients. If you require a winning team – and who doesn't? – you'll need to make some tough decisions about what's already in place and what needs to change.

Starting without a clean sheet is far from easy. My advice here is begin as if you are starting from scratch. Would you have the same people and processes in place? I suspect not. If you've just joined the company, in that you're in charge, you'll have a window to change things. If you're not in that happy position, you might need to create some sort of event as a background for getting things done.

Incidentally, most organisations don't like this idea. Evolution, not Monday Revolution, well that's fine but it's not for me. I've seen people move slowly and stick to their knitting until it unravels… In talking to people about their time at the top, I'd say the majority believe they should have acted more radically and much sooner.

With that in mind, let's review a few companies I've worked in, with and observed. As I've already mentioned, I've been involved with many companies in a wide range of markets. These potentially exciting roles were rewarding but occasionally fell a little short in some respects, but that was my naivety.

In one instance, I thought the company in question would welcome my views, but that wasn't the case. At a meeting I asked what I thought was an appropriate question. The chairman was clearly annoyed by my intervention and queried why I always asked difficult questions. I replied I thought that was why I was there. He explained it wasn't.

At Carphone Warehouse I couldn't help but be impressed by the high-performance executive team. Having known Sir Charles Dunstone, the entrepreneurial founder, for many years I shouldn't have been too surprised. A great combination of vision, tenacity and charm. And a lot more beside. His hirings, promotions and leadership were present at the board and he rarely put a foot wrong. From the finance director to everyone else, these people were on top of their game. Many were long-standing trusted employees who had bought into Charles and his vision for the business, many years before.

Charles was unfailingly loyal and supportive. I recall his description of a meeting in Silicon Valley to secure exclusive distribution of the first iPhone for his shops. He told the board that this was, without question, a victory for the team and he had simply attended to oil the wheels. He displayed complete modesty for every success and without exception credited his winning team. Yet when disaster struck, which occasionally happened, he would take the entire blame for whatever had occurred. He displayed this loyalty to all around him, including longstanding suppliers he regarded as close as those on the payroll of his company.

Having built teams of my own I've reached several conclusions which I think are worth sharing. Whether recruiting from scratch or identifying existing executives, there are rules to follow that will greatly improve the chance of success.

I met a business school professor conducting research into what made a successful business executive. Particularly those who had made it to the top of an organisation. What characteristics did they possess and how could they be identified? Interestingly, there was only one that shone through consistently. A common thread that if discovered in a candidate should start ringing alarm bells in a good way.

Adversity in early life regularly appeared in the research sample as the characteristic that was present in successful candidates. This came in many different ways, from disabling accidents to the early demise of a parent or sibling. And many examples you wouldn't ever wish on your enemies, others or yourself. Yet from a difficult beginning, certain people seem to draw strength from often impossible situations. Perhaps their resolve is driven by an unexplained determination to fight back against the odds. They couldn't help what had happened to them, but they could try to take control of their lives. Using the strength they'd discovered in adversity to drive themselves forward. What doesn't kill you…

In identifying high-performing team members, look for examples of overcoming personal challenges. Delve into their early life and see if anything is there. What have they encountered that they had to conquer? What personal adversity have they had to cope with, win through and overcome? How did they deal with significant events that required them to find resolve they didn't know they possessed? At interviews we tend to concentrate on positives. Successful strategies, achievement of targets, profitable results. But what are the underlying untold stories that drove the determination? To go the extra mile, to refuse to be beaten, we need to find out.

We all know apparently smart capable people who suck the life out of you, and just about everybody else. Riddled with complex hang-ups, they seem able to find issues with every idea. These people have no place at the top table. We need people who inject life and vitality into the workplace. Not recklessly optimistic, but people who seek out answers to problems, who've demonstrated alternative thinking. A track record in getting things done. Gathering evidence for these types of individuals can be challenging, but it's essential and needs to be done diligently.

But luckily, help is at hand. There are people and methods available to assist in making these critical decisions. Think about it this way. The cost of hiring or promoting the wrong person is absolutely enormous. So much is easily disguised at interviews – how do you really know who you're taking on? I've experienced situations where well-meaning business colleagues recommend people only to find they were completely unsuitable. I discuss recruitment elsewhere in the book, but I'll repeat a couple of points or so here.

Building a top team is so important that you need to manage the process at every stage. This is not about delegating a brief to HR or a search firm. It's about spending time with these people, so they know exactly what you require. Early in my management career, when I was first trusted to hire and manage people, I found the whole process of recruitment daunting. Yet now I can point to some significant successes. By that I mean people I hired who have gone on to very senior roles in other organisations.

Within the company I worked in at the time was an executive who had worked in business administration but shown an interest in working in the area of HR. Particularly hiring and development. She was interested in the psychological side of people. What drove them, what were their strengths and weaknesses, and how could you tell? We decided our division could justify a dedicated resource (her, basically) to lead our recruitment drive. Not working in some remote central function, she had working knowledge of how we operated, what we needed and the time pressures we were under.

In order to ensure she had the right tools for the job, we sent her on some expensive training to get her up to speed. This paid dividends. Armed with psychometric testing tools, her formidable EQ and judgement, she ran our recruitment mission to hire the very best we could. And it worked beyond our expectation. It played a major part in the success of the company. I could go as far as to say it was the most critical factor.

Some years after she'd left to have a family, I secured a new role in a company, which unsurprisingly didn't have a person like her. I remember calling her, when she was expecting her second child, and persuading her to help. As soon as she agreed, I drove to her house and gave her a box of CVs from my car boot to get on with! Eventually she joined the company and ended up as corporate communications director, a very talented person.

It's clear. Do not fall into the trap of "it's so hard to find good people". Of course it is if you go about it the wrong way. But if you can develop and hone your methods, tailor-make your processes and hire someone with the right skills, you'll crack it. This is how you identify the people to compete for a place in your high-performance team.

Critical to successful high-performance team building is creating unity and common purpose. Carphone Warehouse was successful because Charles and his business partner David Ross had a vision for a company that didn't yet exist. It was risky, exciting and if successful would be a brand leader and make its founders and early team members extremely wealthy. Sharing that mission, explaining everyone's role and getting their commitment provides the unity and common purpose a team needs to win. It transcends politics, useless meetings, vanity projects and the like.

When the team meets, it's to discuss recent progress and next steps. Actions are shared and supported by everyone, mistakes owned and successes credited. Nothing gets in the way of the need to move forward. Openness and trust are a given in this environment. Good communication is the foundation because everyone needs to know. That's how high-performance teams are built *The Monday Revolution* way.

At Capital Radio it was along these lines. Every Monday we met at 8.30 am to review key decisions and check progress. The meeting never lasted an hour and we didn't need minutes, action points or any of the usual and often unnecessary administration. We always spent a few minutes on finance and sales, the backdrop to everything. Our mission was to build and own the UK's largest UK radio business, measured by audiences, revenue, profit and company valuation. Our cash would only be invested in this plan and we would test everything against our strategy and financial model.

At this meeting were the finance director, operations director, commercial director and strategy director. We employed several hundred people across the UK in multiple locations. Managing the day-to-day was no simple task and could easily have swamped our thinking, as it does for many executives. But on Mondays at least we pushed on with the big picture plan. The board expected it, our investors wanted it and we were very well incentivised to deliver, which we did. That's what top teams are capable of, prioritising and balancing what needs to be achieved, by when. Around our table nobody ever said they were too busy, or it wasn't their job. Never.

Of course, without leadership there's a danger that not too much will get done. At the top table the leader needs to set the agenda and make sure what's agreed actually happens. Unity and shared responsibility are integral parts of success, but someone has to steer the ship, take responsibility and be held to account. I remember being told by my team that they thought in key discussions I remained too quiet for too long. If only I'd made my views known much earlier, it would prevent others promoting their ideas or remedies that would subsequently be kicked into the long grass.

This was not without merit and certainly at times I have been guilty of being too quiet for too long. But I've seen the other side of the argument. Waiting for the boss to go first is always a mistake. Of course, if you're uncertain yourself and are looking for a lead that can be kind of fine. But the extremes are a self-opinionated leader who doesn't listen and has surrounded him or herself with a bunch of sycophants.

Personally, I like letting the team go first and holding my own position in reserve. This can work well on several levels. I may not know the answer, which may be something where specialist knowledge is required, or I'm simply unsure before hearing the views of others. In any event, I believe good leadership at the top table invites views, listens carefully and respectfully, then summarises. With the objective of reaching a team consensus all can support and back.

It doesn't always go that way of course because it isn't always possible to find mutual agreement. In those instances, the leader makes a call explaining their reasons and rationale. Then it's time to move on.

The Monday Revolution (you can start on Monday)

1. Everything from company image to the job described needs to be compelling. To attract the right people, you need to be attractive.
2. The selection process needs to be rigorous and appropriate to what's required. Set tasks. Use outside expertise and tools. Dig deep.
3. Adversity and failure are often hidden drivers of future success.
4. High-performance teams need high-performance leadership. Create the right environment and provide competitive pay and performance rewards linked directly to team and personal achievement.
5. Be a company that everybody aspires to work for and great talent will gravitate towards your organisation.

NUMBERS
PASS THE SPREADSHEET
NUMBERS, IT'S A GAME YOU KNOW
I'M NOT PAYING THAT
BLACK HOLES

Chapter 6
Numbers, it's a game you know

Measurement matters

I had a coffee with someone I hadn't seen in a while and asked how she was doing. She'd started her own business a couple of years ago and 12 months previously told me it was flying. The answer this time was not so positive. "I think I've plenty of customers but I'm not sure I'm making any money," came the response. "I'll not know until the end of the year when my accountant tells me. I'm a bit worried, I don't seem to have much cash in the bank."

Do you ever come across a business you just know isn't going to make it? It happens all the time. In fact, the odds of a new business still being around after five years are less than likely.

Yet so much failure is avoidable. Because the reasons and remedies are often within our control. The evidence we need to succeed is there, but we haven't identified it, organised it or acted on it.

The majority of companies don't make it because of issues with finance which, had they taken the right advice, could have been solved. As we know, financial problems aren't limited to early-stage companies. Every year there are corporate disasters that involve huge national or global organisations. Run by directors who are often paid millions to get it right. As documented in a couple of other chapters, I've worked for businesses that failed to recognise the ship was about to crash onto the rocks.

If you don't have a profitable business model, sooner or later, you'll run out of money. By profitable I mean one that generates more cash than it needs to operate. Profits alone are not a proxy for success due to the financial acrobatics that can be performed in spite of the best efforts of regulators, auditors and those paid to ensure danger is avoided.

My friend running her company didn't know if her business was capable of generating net cash. In the excitement of starting, buying and running a business, many people find the whole area of finance just too… well, boring.

Building a fast-growing business is an exciting challenge. In many cases the founders, unsurprisingly, focus their energies on their vision. Unfortunately, the numbers are often left to take care of themselves.

Whatever business we're in, we need profitable sales. By that we mean the difference between the cost of goods or services, our operating costs and the final selling price. It's no good just concentrating on volume if it doesn't result in net cash to the bottom line.

Early-stage companies often manage their own books with an accountant who prepares the year-end numbers. A bookkeeper is often an early appointment, taking over duties such as monthly accounts, tax, payroll and invoicing.

As a business grows, it employs some regular qualified accountancy help. Often a freelance individual who is acting finance director to several companies steps in, bringing experience and expertise. Eventually this role becomes permanent, as does the need for a well-resourced accountancy firm who will advise on best practice.

But beware. There is a significant variance in quality, and the type of help you get will make an enormous difference to whether you succeed or fail. Do your due diligence thoroughly before making an appointment. Understand your business model and keep your new advisors on a very short leash until you're confident they're right for you.

The rule here for business owners, large and small, is understand your own numbers. Have the best you can afford to provide regular financial information and never fail to act on what you know. If your company would benefit from a weekly cash flow report, get it done and use it. Buy financial support you can grow into.

There's plenty on offer, but it's not all the same, so take time to select the best you can afford. Even if that means diverting expenditure from elsewhere. Of course, a new website is far more exciting than hiring a new accountant. But you really won't enjoy the excitement of running out of cash and going bust.

The business owner found the help she needed, survived and is doing well. Because early on she recognised the urgency for financial skills she didn't have but needed. Elsewhere I've talked about being on top of the numbers as a core responsibility for everyone. In larger organisations there's always the danger of assumption – in that someone else is in charge so you don't really need to pay too much attention. Beware.

The Monday Revolution (you can start on Monday)

1. Recognise that, ultimately, having no cash is the only reason companies fail.
2. Avoid running out of cash by staying very, very close to the numbers.
3. Invest in financial resources you trust and ensure your management reports match the business needs. A company I work with has a daily cash flow tracker. Not a bad idea.
4. If sales dip beyond your expectation, have a back-up plan. Defer expenditure. Negotiate better payment terms. Put "exciting" projects on hold. Be prepared to fire people in extreme circumstances.
5. Most companies leave it far too late to take action. Relying on "I hope it gets better". By the time they bite the bullet the situation has started to spiral out of control. Don't be one of those.

Chapter 7
Pass the spreadsheet
Data. Wood. Data. Trees. Data.

It really wasn't so long ago that we didn't seem to have enough information. At least it was hard to locate as the world's information was highly disseminated in libraries, universities and countless other places. If only we could collect more data and acquire more knowledge, we'd all make better, more informed decisions.

We've moved from limited information to unlimited information in a very, very short period of time. And working out what to do with what we have is a competitive challenge. Competitive because chances are our competition have what we have. Not our confidential information private to us but plenty of public information and bespoke commissioned information of their own.

How we assimilate information and organise it into reports that are management tools is key to making progress. Documents are produced for all sorts of valid reasons and should be a useful aid to decision making.

I sit around some management meetings where the reports are clear, brief and provide useful written commentary. They bring everyone up to speed and the business benefits as a result. New reports are provided but there is a strict understanding that we could easily drown in operational detail, so everything is challenged for relevance and whether the report is just for interest (out it goes) or actionable.

As previously mentioned, I was a great admirer of Carphone Warehouse, an international business, grown from scratch, with a top management team. At the board meetings the executives always appeared to be very much on top of their business divisions and I was constantly impressed by their grasp of the key issues.

The more challenging area for me was the information distributed before the meeting. Mostly a compilation of management reports and accounts with little explanation to the occasional attender of meetings, such as myself. I think it took me at least two years to persuade them that an executive summary would help me (and perhaps them) focus on the important things to discuss. As a non-executive director it wasn't my role to know everything, far from it. What I needed was a simple report that summarised business performance and the key areas we needed to talk about.

Rather like meetings, reports take on a life of their own – the original intention of the document having been long forgotten. They tend to expand as executives suggest new areas to look at. "Wouldn't it be useful if we could have the average order value ranked by customer sector?" It could be a great decision, of course. But it will be layered on top of the existing information which, very likely, will remain. And that's the problem. When were you last in a meeting where someone challenged the existing regularly produced reports and suggested they should be culled?

I've often suggested information could be easily summarised into key points and we could just read those and then discuss.

That's my preferred way of dealing with information. Short and to the point.

In fact, I like to apply that to all my business dealings where possible. In my advisory role I don't offer to write reports. I very specifically say that if you need me to solve a problem, I'll willingly take a look. But if you require a detailed report, that isn't me. I'll give a short summary and talk to you about what I've found and what I'd do if I was you. For some that has limited appeal and those projects rightly go to someone else.

As I was advised many years ago: "Don't offer to write reports, no one ever reads them. If they want something on paper talk to them and they can write it down." Of course, there are important situations where written reports are mandatory. You wouldn't want a thorough analysis of your IT system delivered verbally. Definitely not.

Like most things in *The Monday Revolution*, it's a judgement call. My point is simply that too much information is a constraint, not a help. Businesses that have a few ground rules about how information is collected and produced in reports are more likely to flourish. They make better decisions more quickly. Like many aspects in life, the collectors and assimilators of information focus on their priorities and areas of interest, not always those of the intended recipient. That leaves people like me searching through the document trying to identify the things that really matter. Or looking for an important point we know should be in there somewhere.

Therefore, it's not surprising the ubiquitous, good old KPI, made a welcome appearance many years ago. And from what I can see, has bred very well as the amount of instantly accessible data ballooned. The demand for data analysis continues to grow as we collect significant amounts of information about each other.

In some respects, the emphasis has shifted from who has the base data to who has the best systems for dealing with it. I know of two competing companies who have the same information, but one is growing far quicker than the other. Why? Because the accelerating company has developed algorithms that provide forecast customer purchase behaviour. The other simply hasn't and is desperately trying to catch up.

The Monday Revolution (you can start on Monday)

1. Acknowledge that too much information overwhelms people and can restrict productivity and growth.
2. Clever analysis of data is undoubtedly a competitive edge, providing it's actionable. In a world that shares the same information, it's what you do with it that your competitors don't that counts.
3. What do you have, what do you need and what are you doing with it?
4. Reduce the amount of KPIs. You know you've already too many to make sense of all of them.

Chapter 8
I'm not paying that
The price is right?

How much does price matter to your business? How often do you review your pricing strategies to achieve the optimum relationship between sales and making a profit?

Management of manufactured products will apply the "cost plus" method to generate a margin and test it against competing brands. Retailers, whether high street or based online, compete ferociously on price and try to maintain their margins by passing on price cuts to their suppliers. These tend to get passed back up the supply chain, often resulting in losses for some.

Retailers understand pricing psychology better than most. They have the ability to test strategies and develop sophisticated approaches to determine what to charge. They often promote their pricing position, making it central to their marketing to bang the message home. From "Every Little Helps" to the annoyingly clunky "Never Knowingly Undersold". I think it's time the UK retailer John Lewis changed that, as I'm pretty sure it's lost on a lot of people.

I spend much of my time in professional services, where there exists a much more random approach to charging customers. At least that's how it appears. In many sectors there are huge variances in price, and I have come to the conclusion there are lessons that could be learnt from the retail sector. In fact, whatever market you're in, the retail approach to pricing provides examples for everyone.

Many continue to price their services in the way they have since they came into existence, which for some is a very long time. Accountants and lawyers are generally guilty of this approach and will, over time, lose out to new entrants who offer a more transparent pricing model. It's already beginning to happen with new online-only companies springing up. From fixed-rate services making bold moves into the hourly pricing model employed by traditional firms and vice versa. Customers are becoming less tolerant of not really knowing what they are going to pay until the invoice arrives.

I've seen several examples of this lately. In one, the law firm were less than clear what they were going to be charging. They consequently presented a bill that the client was extremely unhappy about and refused to pay. There was an assumption that the customer was aware that as the work was taking longer, a larger bill would arrive. The client believed the longer period was the firm's fault, not his, and thought he'd agreed a fixed price. He paid a reduced amount and swapped law firms.

Someone once said, "A million dollars is the most negotiable number in the world". Whoever they were, they were right. Round numbers never look considered, even in the world of professional services. Yet companies continue to employ their use, oblivious to how much business it might be costing. I've seen clients push back on paying a quoted £10,000 but very happy to go with £9,750. Would a retailer ever charge a round £10 for a product? Unlikely.

I work with one company that has been under-charging their clients for years. Mostly due to their initial misplaced enthusiasm that price would be the deciding factor in awarding a contract (it rarely is). But over time we've worked together to significantly increase prices. We managed this because they provide an excellent service and the clients acknowledged they were underpaying. Of course, it wasn't that straightforward. Every situation was unique and required a different approach to meet the circumstances. But it worked and no client fired us.

Often, we're afraid to charge what we're offering at the price we think it's really worth. Here's a typical conversation:

> "Their budget is around £50K but for the work they want doing we would usually charge £80K. But they could be a long-term client. We could charge them £50K now with an agreement the price increases over time, starting at the next review."

Good idea but rarely works out. And over time you start to resent this client who's paying you far less than most of your other customers.

What to do?

In this case you could offer to schedule the payment terms by deferring some to another year. Not ideal, doesn't help cash flow. Chop some of the services out to match the £50K. Or walk away.

Build into your proposal enough things to sacrifice. Assume everyone will want to chip the price. It's expected. It's important to anticipate how it's likely to play out.

Pricing is a hugely complex subject which I fully intend to address at some future point. In the meantime, have a look at the points below.

The Monday Revolution (you can start on Monday)

1. Collect pricing data for your products and services and think like a retailer.
2. How could you be a price disrupter and avoid disruption through more creative pricing?
3. How can you provide clients with more transparency?
4. What can you do to turn project income into sustainable monthly income?
5. Identify lost leaders, low margins, vanity projects. If they don't pay their way, ditch them.

Chapter 9
Black holes

Disappearing money and how to avoid it

Some people like to keep their finance director in a box at the back of the cupboard. On a lower shelf, in the dark, where occasionally they can be dusted down and taken out to produce some numbers. Others keep them on a short leash to ensure complete obedience. Neither is to be recommended. To the accomplished business leader this sounds ridiculous. *The Monday Revolution* approach to finance is one of ensuring the finance director has an access-all-areas pass and fulfils the role of trusted lieutenant. Complete integrity and independence are required. With the character to blow the whistle on poor practice or suspected criminal activity.

But unfortunately, in spite of best intentions, history proves that we're never too far away from the next financial scandal enveloping a well-known company of some sort or another. Usually involving the finance director who is either incompetent or compliant.

Too often the finance function is regarded as a necessary evil, something that constrains growth not promotes it. As a result, signs get missed. Evidence is conveniently ignored and then there is a day of reckoning where the black hole, that could have been foreseen and avoided, is revealed. At which point the blame is allocated.

Here's an example from a CFO I once interviewed. The organisation he worked for had been bought by a larger one and the chief executive had been summoned to New York to present the budget for the following year. The conversation went something like this:

CFO to the CEO: "Shall we get the early flight to New York?"

CEO: "I've decided you're not joining us, all you'll do is talk about the numbers."

CFO: "Yes but it's a budget meeting."

Anyway, he didn't go. The CEO often kept the finance director away from information and key decisions and this was just another example. The new owner soon grew tired of what had become a disappointing purchase. Its performance fell well short of expectation and the finance director was powerless to help as the chief executive had him well and truly side-lined. The business was sold shortly afterwards.

On another occasion, I was consulting a company where the founders had been reluctant to hire a fully qualified, experienced finance person. Sometimes it's hard to convince founders to hire when they're obsessed with growing sales and not much else. Often, I find they look back wondering how they ever coped, sometimes reflecting that their company could have made better progress had a good finance director been on board.

The reluctant company in question realised they needed to step up when a black hole suddenly appeared. Except saying it was sudden is generous. In fact, it had been slowly growing over a period of months and happened to be revealed when I questioned the accounts in the quarterly management meeting.

As usual all the focus had been on sales, not surprising as this was the founders' background and they'd grown the company into a multimillion-pound business. All the emphasis was on the top line and the company held this metric in esteem above all others. After the usual reports, I asked the finance guy if we could look at cash flow and the balance sheet. Low and thin was how I would describe them.

CEO: "How can this be, we're generating record sales?"

COO: "Indeed. We've never had more customers, we've had to hire more people in customer service to cope with demand."

At last, the finance director spoke up:

"The problem is we've dropped our prices and every new sale loses money when we take into account the cost of servicing the customer. The more sales we win at the wrong price, the more operating cash leaves the building. We have a black hole in the accounts."

Black holes are unexpected debt that needs to be dealt with quickly before it pulls the company into insolvency. In this case it was impossible to cancel unprofitable contracts or raise prices for existing customers at such short notice. Consequently, we delayed future budgeted expenditure, cut costs and borrowed some money. Today the company is healthy and has a new finance director.

Whose fault was that? Well, the naive founders and the finance guy who should have had the right controls in place to ensure all the sales were profitable. His job was to provide management with critical information and a narrative. Their job was to give him the opportunity to explain what was going on and have the sense to listen. They did neither.

Here's *The Monday Revolution* advice I give every executive and every board I'm involved with as a director or advisor: hire a finance person with operational experience and let them loose, everywhere. We hired a new executive at a fast-growing company and I said to the chief executive, tell the entire company this person has an access-all-areas pass. They can and will go wherever they want and ask any questions they like.

At Capital Radio, I learnt the wisdom of this approach. Our finance director was very bright and very capable. We called him the ferret. Exactly. He went everywhere and if something didn't seem right, he sniffed it out. He hired experienced people with similar qualities to his own. Their curiosity, tenacity and authority provided the company with the right information. Armed with this we could make much better evidence-based decisions.

He was naturally cautious and always slightly anxious. The right antidote to an optimistic boss who needed the brakes applied. But we had no black holes and a balanced discussion around operations, investment and risk. I only really appreciated the value of this relationship after I was exposed to other companies whose financial controls were badly organised.

My most disturbing experience was with a board of directors where the finance director was incapable of independent thought and saw fit to produce the numbers the chief executive wanted to see, regardless of how they were arrived at. As sales and margins declined, the company unravelled to the point of no return. This type of behaviour was prevalent in the 1980s, when accounting standards were not what they are today, and companies could "create" profits from what were effectively loss-making businesses. That tradition continued into the 2000s where the collapse of the USA housing market, due to fraudulently traded worthless bonds, cost millions of people their homes and their jobs. The biggest black hole of all time.

The company went bust. Of course it did. Shareholders lost money and the CEO eventually had to sell his house to pay his personal debts. A sorry tale that was entirely avoidable had hubris not prevailed.

Here's another black hole. I'm in some ways reluctant to depress you with further tales of mishap but they do illustrate the need for vigilance. Particularly when your finance person isn't everything you thought they were cracked up to be.

Some years ago, I joined the board of a company that had a sound and reputable business. Or so I thought. I'd hardly finished my induction day before the wheels started to fall off. Profit warnings, a scapegoated discarded chief executive and a board that was not fit for purpose. Why did I join this car crash? Well that's a whole other story. But I'll certainly concede that if I'd been more careful, more diligent and less influenced by others, I'd never have taken the job.

This was a story that has played out many times. Again, it was the finance guy who was at the centre of the problem, but in many respects it wasn't his fault. Newly over-promoted, he was strongly influenced by the chairman and his small cohort of long-serving non-execs. He didn't have time to establish his independence and authority; he was on probation.

"You have to understand this is a cyclical business," the chairman regularly informed his fellow directors.

"Those of us that have seen it before know we will ride the down times and generate significant profits when demand returns."

I respectfully pointed out it didn't look this way to me. The consumer was rapidly moving online where we had little presence in any capacity. And anyway, others in our market had started selling our leading brands at prices we couldn't compete with. Furthermore, our international business in many countries was losing money, in fact, virtually everywhere. And there was a lot of it, as the company had been on an acquisition spree but failed to properly manage these recently gained assets, so most were in various states of disarray.

My concerns were not well received. To compound my unpopularity, I challenged the company's contingency planning suggesting the process fell a long way short of best practice. This was not, in my book, *The Monday Revolution* way of dealing with the immediate issues.

When I reflect on this sorry moment, it's clear what should have taken place to rescue the situation. Like black holes, disruptive changes in markets rarely happen overnight. The signs are usually there a long time in advance but a failure to recognise and acknowledge them leads to long-term decline and a messy end. Often resulting in the company executives desperately seeking a short-term life raft that just leaves them clinging to the wreckage. In these cases, long-term unservice-able debt becomes the creator of the black hole until the bankers call it a day.

There we are. Examples of how black holes can appear in a business universe. And they do, every year. Destroying compa-nies and livelihoods. Rarely criminal offences. Just the result of poor controls and incompetence. If there's a common theme it appears to me, in researching this book, that an overbearing chief executive and weak subordinates, board and chairman are usually at the heart of the problem.

The term *black hole* is relatively new, although their exis-tence is as old as time itself. However old that is I don't know, and neither does anyone else. Black holes have such gravitational pull that once sucked in, nothing can escape. An unexplained void where bad things can happen. Complete darkness where no light can escape; they sit there waiting to be discovered.

For us in business these are self-inflicted events that can, as I have proved, become fatal if not discovered, acknowledged and dealt with quickly. And as we've discussed, many people at the top are responsible for creating the circumstances that help them flourish.

This can be done in a covert way to disguise falling perfor-mance. Such as an aggressive approach to capitalising expen-diture. "Look, our computers will last five years not three and while we're at it we can spread the cost of many items over several years to improve the profits." And many other scams, far more complicated, designed to baffle investors and convince the world all is well. Moving liabilities off the balance sheet out of view has brought many companies crashing down.

Of course, auditing firms are there to protect shareholders against this type of aggressive accounting and I've been present at many audit meetings and watched the CFO argue his case for flattering the numbers. In some instances, the auditors just completely miss the problem. The business eventually implodes, often triggered by a whistleblower, prompting shareholders and regulators to look for who to blame.

Although this is an all-too-frequent occurrence, it is rare the auditors suffer too much, mostly citing the evidence that has come to light was hidden from them and couldn't be taken into account. In the crash of 2008, no CFO or CEO was prosecuted for wrong behaviour and most kept their extraordinarily high compensation in spite of presiding over the worst financial meltdown since the Great Depression.

So, there we have it, black holes. From the small company to a global catastrophe. All share similar traits. Senior people who chose to look away. Weak systems and controls. A reliance on people not qualified to be in charge and dominant leaders who intimidated any financial challenge.

The Monday Revolution recognises a simple truth. The most important number in any business is cash. Everything a business does ultimately has to generate cash above any other financial measure. If you're spending more cash than you can make you will go bust. See above.

Here's the good news. You can mostly avoid all this in your world. It's not always easy because it requires commitment, diligence and an enquiring disposition. This is one occasion where there is a point to having a dog and barking yourself.

The Monday Revolution (you can start on Monday)

1. Do not cut corners when hiring finance people. Find the best you can, validate with supporting evidence and pay them well.
2. Sit them at the top of the company. Involve them in strategy and operations; they need to know everything.
3. Make it clear they can go anywhere and ask anything, of anybody, including you.
4. Ensure they recognise they are ultimately accountable for all financial evidence. Discuss the potential of black holes.
5. Always understand cash flow.

Chapter 10
A sales story or two
No sales, no business

I'm told some products sell themselves, but I've never had the good fortune to work with one of those companies. I think I've probably encountered every sort of sales challenge. And although every business is different, in truth there probably are less than a dozen hurdles to get over, whatever market they're in. From identifying and connecting with the decision maker to a superior competitor selling their products at a loss to win market share. And every other pitfall in between, awaiting the intrepid deal closer!

A common negative among buyers is "there's no budget". It's been cut, spent, diverted, reallocated or some such plausible reason that means your products will definitely not be on the purchase list. I learnt by experience (no sales and no commission) that what people say isn't necessarily the end of the matter. In fact, rather than fearing the worst, I would relish the challenge of "no budget".

Back in the nineties, an advertising space salesman from a TV company was in France watching Jaguar win the 24-hour Le Mans race. Although not a huge fan of the sport, as a guest he'd been grateful for the invitation. Much to his surprise, he found the whole event captivating and the experience stayed with him long after he returned to the UK.

A few months later he was in the offices of JWT, the Jaguar advertising agency, trying to win new business. After discussing the active campaigns, he enquired after their client, Jaguar, noting how they'd triumphed in France a few months before.

The JWT executive was less than interested.

"To be honest they don't really do much advertising and certainly not on TV. Anyway, there's no budget for consumer advertising; they're really concentrating on their dealer network."

The salesman tried his best, but the JWT guy was keen to get to lunch. A key part of the day for advertising people in those times.

Our salesman remembered the glory of the race. What a proud moment for Jaguar owners and the all-important dealer network. And then he came up with a compelling idea to generate money from the apparently non-existent budget.

As the advertising agency were likely to be less than helpful, he contacted the marketing director of Jaguar and tried to secure an appointment on the basis that he had a special idea. The director wanted a written approach before agreeing to meet, but our man explained that he needed just 30 minutes to demonstrate his game-changing idea. Part cynical, part intrigued, the marketing director fixed the meeting. He thought it would probably come to nothing but other than time there wasn't much to lose.

When the advertising agency discovered their client was being directly approached, they were less than pleased. They made it clear again to the salesman that TV advertising was absolutely not on the agenda. There was no interest from their point of view. And anyway, as they'd already made clear, no budget. As their executive said:

> "If you want to waste your time on a 200-mile round trip to Coventry, that's your problem."

The salesman wasn't put off. He believed his idea was compelling and that presented in the right way, a budget would be found. Prior to the meeting he'd asked the guys in production to make a three-minute advertisement for Jaguar featuring footage from their 24-hour Le Mans winning race. The voice-over extolled the virtues of Jaguar, utilising the messages they were using in their current trade advertising. He created a mini version of the prime-time news show and placed the advertisement as the only one in the middle of the programme.

Armed with his video he waited for the marketing director to enter the meeting room. It was a cordial but business-like start. Clearly the director wanted to get to the point quickly, but the salesman wasn't about to be rushed. They discussed Jaguar's marketing plan, the key messages and the dealers' need to feel supported.

The salesman set the scene. He said his idea worked at two levels. A high-impact one-off TV feature, which would be a much-talked-about event by Jaguar owners and potential buyers. It would be pre-marketed to the dealer network as a sign of great confidence and commitment, helping them sell more cars. This was unique, because no one company had ever had exclusivity for their own advertisement in the centre break of the flagship premier news programme.

Then he played the video. The director was non-committal: "Show me again." The salesman played it a second time and waited. The director turned to him, stretched his arms out as if to embrace the screen and said: "This is Jaguar."

The salesman and the director discussed budgets and timings. The director said there was no budget for the opportunity, but the idea was so strong that it couldn't be passed by or risked being sold in some way to a competitor.

Not surprisingly, the agency quickly fell into line and the advertisement ran to great applause from customers, dealers and the media. The agency collected an industry award for "their" great idea and the media salesman had no trouble seeing their clients in the future! Studying what a company is trying to achieve is key. If you want to significantly improve your chances, understand their priorities. It's about their needs, not about yours.

The Monday Revolution requires a positive mindset. This idea was a good one and in spite of detractors the salesman believed in it. As if it was his responsibility to sell Jaguar cars.

Remember, budgets are a management tool, usually set annually. For many they provide a barrier to flexible thinking. People hide behind "there's no budget" but in truth there is always a budget for a great idea. Middlemen and gatekeepers are not always your friend. Upsetting them is unwise, but occasionally you need to go around them, or over them. Do this carefully. Identify the decision maker and present the reason for meeting as a compelling and unique event. Our salesman's goal was to sell the marketing director advertising space. If he'd said that at the outset, the meeting would never have taken place.

The following is another example of overcoming a barrier to meeting; I was told this tale by a highly successful executive. His technique to securing high-level meetings was simple but required the confidence of upfront investment. He provided unique information as a means of reaching his target prospects.

It worked something like this. "We've just conducted a study on the market outlook for your sector and some of the results are rather surprising. Would you like to see the data?" This approach to relationship building is a classic way of getting in front of someone. If they ask for an email first, send them a teaser.

Information is a certain way of meeting buyers across all sectors. Conferences, seminars and networking events all rely on gathering customer prospects together, by providing something they don't possess and isn't easily available anywhere else. They need to know because their competitors might get ahead of them and in any case it could further their own knowledge and prospects.

I've worked for many professional service companies, such as accountants and lawyers. They are extremely good at running seminars attended by current clients (adds value to the relationship) and future prospects. These magnets work well by providing updates, new information or the organising company's view on what new legislation, for example, might bring. What they're generally pretty poor at is converting that short-term goodwill into a fee-paying client. But that's covered in another chapter.

It may sound like a harsh observation, but people will only be interested in meeting you, in a business sense at least, if you can provide something of value that will help them. You might baulk at this but why else should they bother? In a busy time-constrained world, why waste your valuable executive paid-for time on a meeting that might go nowhere? After all, a key theme of *The Monday Revolution* is investing time wisely and that doesn't just apply to you!

I recognise that there's a convention that says meeting someone for a cup of coffee and chewing things over can be useful. Maybe. But if you want to generate sales and profits it's a long-winded way of going about it. Personally, it's become a reduced part of my strategy.

I've always positioned my commercial approaches to people I don't know as one that respects their time. I wouldn't contact them for a cosy chat. "I have something that should be of genuine interest. Give me a short meeting slot and I'll show you the benefits."

If you know your market, you'll be very aware of any information shortfalls. And you can fill the gap by satisfying that need. Of course, you're not there simply to provide free data. It's a catalyst for reviewing their products, brands, reputation, image, whatever. And your product can provide the answers once you've probed, questioned and above all listened intelligently.

The result of these types of meetings will virtually always be positive if you've done your homework. You're building a relationship and as a result the onus will be on you to fix a further discussion and provide some kind of proposal or plan. It may be a lengthy road to closing a deal but you're on the way and will have made very important early steps.

As a basic principle, having something others need and don't have is of great value. In my advisory company virtually all our work comes from personal recommendation. But in the early days we needed to convince people we didn't know why they should be interested in meeting us.

In order to grow our company, we were out and about meeting people who we thought we could help. My business partners (more subtle than me!) used to squirm at some of my sales approaches at conferences, parties or other events.

"Hi, I'm David from The Drive Partnership, good to meet you, how's your week going?"

After some small talk I'd engineer the conversation around to the sort of thing we do for our clients.

"What exactly does The Drive Partnership do?" they would ask.

The earlier opening conversation would have shaped my response. But typically, I'd say something like this:

"We work with companies helping them hit their growth targets more quickly than they can on their own. Basically, they just get there sooner after they've hired us."

"Really, how do you do that?"

"Well, it depends on the organisation but often they just need more profitable clients. We help them achieve that aim, usually quite quickly. Would that interest you or are you OK in that department?"

At this point the person is usually interested enough to agree to a short meeting to hear more. No need for us to go into detail. Mission accomplished. A diary date is arranged, and a deal gets done. Our early clients are still with us years later. As one says:

"David is the most commercial person I know. He's our business advisor and we don't make any major decisions without consulting him."

I'm honoured and flattered by that. Having a seat at the top table is a great responsibility and not without its challenges of course. It all started by being interested in his company at a drinks party a long time ago…

The Monday Revolution (you can start on Monday)

1. Information and ideas are gold if you have something that others will perceive as valuable.
2. Spend time looking at the company's activity, profile and market. Work out what you could provide. This may just cost you time. Available public data highlighting trends could be all you need.
3. Make what you have unique. Even if it's collated from the point above. It can be your insightful take on the data or creative idea.
4. Having secured a meeting, the aim is to uncover the client's unsolved problems and carefully match your proposition. Always leave with agreed actions to follow up. Always.
5. If you're networking, listen and say enough to agree a follow-up. Resist the temptation to hit the sales pitch button.

Chapter 11
Right message, right place, right time
Making the most of marketing money

W e've moved on from the famous quote of "half my adver-
tising budget is wasted but I don't know which half". In that the arrival of multi-digital channels has provided much higher levels of accountability of cause and effect.

Even so, measuring sales as a result of spending marketing money is tricky, but great if you can do it. But not everybody can. It remains a complex area and, in many respects, still requires better analysis to ensure money is spent in the right place, at the right time, with a compelling story or message.

And what happens when company budgets are tight and there's a need to make savings? There are places to head for to unlock short-term profits or losses. And the marketing budget often holds the key. Why would this important line of expenditure offer itself up for a cut?

Well, you wouldn't cut anything that you could readily attribute to sales or profits, would you? But in many companies marketing expenditure often lacks accountability. It's seen as a cost, not an investment, and the relationship between spending the money and gaining a return is often distant to say the least.

No wonder the proponents of this important function occasionally leave the budget meeting disappointed.

The Monday Revolution is here to help!

Some organisations like to back weight (spend in the last quarter of the year if possible) so the planned money can be grabbed back for the bottom line if the year has been tougher than forecast. Smart finance people never lose sight of unspent money and keep a running check of what might be reclaimed. And there's no issue with that.

Back in the day, marketing money (advertising if you like) was spent and accountable at varying levels. If the money was spent and directly attributable to sales it was protected. Advertising a coded special offer that could be tracked and measured would be a good example.

Image advertising tended to attract the big budgets but was often measured on "awareness" and "attitudinal studies". Disciples of these budgets (usually advertising agencies in their various forms) promoted this along the lines of "if people haven't heard of your brand, they're far less likely to buy it".

Others would point out that while the argument was logical, spending millions to generate awareness and imagery was far too removed from the effect on future sales and profits. In challenging times these budgets commonly found their way back to the savings account.

Much has been written about the allocation of marketing monies. Studies and case histories are frequently produced, mostly by those having a vested interest in some capacity. Back in 1980 Simon Broadbent, an advertising guru who used a slide rule (look it up) for calculations, produced an authoritative book *Spending Advertising Money* together with his colleague

Brian Jacobs. At the time this was seen as an influential work to treat marketing money as an investment not a donation.

In the world of consumer products, advertising and marketing plays a crucial role in the development of establishing a brand and selling it profitably. As a salesman in the 1970s, I was selling confectionary to multiple and independent retailers in London and the south of the UK.

Television advertising always had a dramatic effect on my sales figures. Often, the retailer would refuse to stock a line if it wasn't supported with a media spend. If our competitors were advertising and we weren't, we'd find our products pushed to the back of the store. Or at worst taken off the approved purchase list.

In my book, all money spent on advertising has to earn its keep. It may not be easy to untangle the various forms of complementary promotional activity but that doesn't mean we shouldn't try. Of course, it may be several combined courses of action that result in improved sales and singling out each one for cause and effect is a bit tricky. But that shouldn't stop what is a critical exercise.

I've always found consumer marketing easier and more dynamic. By easy I mean easier than, say, a business advertising to another business.

Reaching business decision makers is always challenging. Who are they? How do you get in front of them with your image and product? What are their decision-making rules and how can you find out?

I've worked with many companies whose biggest frustration is being relatively unknown and the first jump they have to make is explaining who they are and what they do. Always a challenging place to be. When I advise business companies seeking new clients, I always ask: "Who's heard of you and why should they be interested in what you're selling? What problem are you solving?"

Incredibly, executives, many in high places, struggle to answer these three questions. Companies need to go back to basics and address the fundamental questions of what to do, when and why. Marketing should be treated as an accountable discipline, not easily junked because it can't be justified. Or undercapitalised because it isn't recognised as a driver of profitable sales. That requires it being subject to a routine disciplined review, evidence based.

Let's consider how one might manage marketing investment, in that there is a lot of available data, which is helpful and can be used to great effect. If you're working in a business without information, you need to find some, otherwise it's impossible to make evidence-based decisions.

Everyone interested in reaching consumers sells on a multi-channel basis: high street stores, shopping centres, events and online. Even some companies that started out online are looking for a physical presence. Amazon are opening unmanned cash-free stores and there's no doubt this blended model will be the way forward for many.

Marketing money is a precious resource, not to be wasted. Here's how a review led to a controversial but ultimately better use of funds...

Clare wasn't particularly looking forward to the board meeting. Presenting to a group of seasoned directors and her colleagues was surely an opportunity to demonstrate she was at the top of her game. Except that wasn't how she felt.

In today's retail market the future is less than clear. Online sales were growing, but not enough to match the fall of those in the high street stores. Clare was responsible for hundreds of outlets selling consumer durables, from toasters to laptops, and expected to grow the business. Yet these days just matching last year's numbers seemed like a positive result.

Clare knew that the difference between a good year and a bad one is the Christmas sales peak and the weeks that follow. A good year can be wrecked by failing to get it right in the last calendar quarter.

Every year the same strategy was used to drive shoppers into her stores. Some unique products that could only be bought in those outlets, coupled with attractive discounts and payment terms. And snowmen and tinsel in the windows.

Yet Clare felt something was missing. Change was needed to tip the balance of success in the company's favour. She decided to meet with her colleagues to review plans and not just repeat last year's formula. There must be a way to generate more business, not involving even more marketing money and deeper discounts. Both of which would very likely hit profitability.

The meeting explored the reasons for not selling more product. Everything from supply chain issues to competitive pricing. They agreed factors such as the economy, the weather and other matters were outside their control. Other than having a reactionary plan there was little they could do.

As the discussion progressed Clare realised what needed to be done. It would be a radical approach, but it was logical and based on indisputable evidence. There was a clear problem, that if successfully addressed, would lift sales and win customers. In fact, it would create more loyal shoppers, perhaps for years to come.

The thought of presenting this new approach at the board was daunting. What if they considered her strategy was poorly thought through? Would her job be at risk? Clare knew it might be and certainly would be if Christmas sales missed the target. But in spite of sleepless nights she decided to press ahead.

Clare was allocated 20 minutes at the meeting to present her plans. The board members liked Clare and always looked forward to her attending. But they were very aware that the market had been challenging and that improvements needed to be made. Not least of all to appease the company's shareholders who were becoming grumpy at the faltering sales line and falling share price. Everything was hanging on a successful Christmas; everyone knew that.

Clare's moment arrived. She wasted no time in explaining that a successful trading period needed more than glitzy TV advertising and snowmen in the windows. It needed a new look at how to sell more product, but at no additional cost.

Clare asked them a question: "What percentage of people who visit our stores actually buy something?"

Selling electronic consumer products is not an easy business. It takes time to explain and help the customer decide on the right product, particularly at a time of the year when most purchases are gifts.

Everyone widely overestimated the right answer of 13%. Consequently, 87% of potential purchasers were leaving the shops empty-handed.

Clare explained her plan. Why was the company spending millions on TV marketing and promotion? Surely that just made the problem worse? Why drive more people into crowded stores where we can't serve them? Resulting in frustrated customers and stressed staff.

Why not significantly reduce the marketing activity and invest the money in hiring and training new people? Presumably less customers would come to the stores, enabling them to serve and sell to those who were there. In addition, she would focus on promoting items that provided a decent margin but could be quickly sold off the shelf. The company would sell to a higher percentage of their shoppers and provide a better service, creating a better experience and more loyalty.

Whether on or offline, business has always been about "conversion". Generating high volumes of customers is pointless if they don't make a purchase. It sounds counterintuitive to want fewer customers. But businesses would make much more money by better-targeted advertising aimed at people who are far more likely to buy something. The lesson is to have a joined-up approach to marketing and connected sales. Too often there's a gap between marketing investment and purchasing.

Clare presented a detailed financial analysis to support her new ideas. It wasn't rocket science. Just recognition of the facts and a simple plan that had every chance of working. The board agreed the strategy and Clare was delighted and somewhat relieved.

Average customer conversion increased by 30%, and in some stores it was even higher. No one could argue with that improvement! Margins increased too as did overall sales volume and customer satisfaction levels. All in all, a good example of examining the data and having the courage to make an evidence-based decision. Good work, Clare.

The Monday Revolution (you can start on Monday)

1. Is marketing money seen as a nice-to-have or an essential driver of sales?
2. Do you account for marketing money as an investment? Is expenditure expected to generate a measurable return? If not, why not?
3. Review plans every time. It's just too easy to repeat last time's activity.

Chapter 12
We made the shortlist!

Improving the odds of winning a pitch

At some point, everybody gets involved in pitching for business. A new contract. A new position or promotion. Back office or front line. Production, services or accounts. The process touches everyone directly or indirectly.

> "It was close, very close. You came a very worthy second and if it doesn't work out with the other guys we'll be back. Please pass on my thanks to all the team that pitched."

So say many executives when delivering disappointing news to the losers.

Of course, the best position to create is one where there's no pitch at all. Having built a relationship already, why would the client or prospect want to put themselves through the pain of a selection process, only to appoint a company they already know and trust? And of course, that's the optimum for any company trying to secure extra business. Getting themselves in the right position for new or more work. But we'll come to that shortly.

Let's begin with the classic starting position from both sides. The client needs to hire a new agency, advisor, IT specialist, whatever. Often there's groupthink and debate here as to what's required. Perhaps it's related to a new venture or a current supplier who, for some reason, is just not up to scratch. Somebody is charged with writing the specification to capture what's required.

Good idea of course. Unless the decision makers have now delegated to someone whose job it is to interpret the thinking with their own well-intentioned interpretation. A sort of "Chinese whispers" enters the process, and unless checked can very easily lead to a distorted brief, with all the important emphasis in the wrong place. This can easily happen and before you know it, the wrong priorities enter the process.

On the other hand, the specification can be spot on and a clear guide to those planning to emerge victorious. Often, the company involved will have a well-worn path to follow. An invitation to get involved, followed up with a Request for Proposal (RFP) and an offer of a call or meeting to answer initial questions.

Having been on both sides of this many times I'm more than guilty of the many crimes that result in a suboptimal decision. As the purchaser of services, I often failed to give it my full attention and didn't really think what I thought until the point of decision. By that time a lot of people had attempted to interpret my thinking, but I hadn't made it easy. Displaying obvious disinterest, leaving others to make it happen in my absence.

Much as we probably all like to think we operate consensual, decision-making machines, more junior executives usually don't want to make an appointment of any magnitude if the business leader is clearly not on side. Particularly if they're the kind of leader who'll always remember they didn't like it when you did. I hope I learnt from that over time; I'm sure I did. You're on a hiding to nothing when the most senior person in the room openly disagrees with what you want to do but tells you to go ahead anyway. Always ends in tears (yours).

I still work with very senior executives who go through the pretence of delegation or display disinterest only to make their feelings known at the eleventh hour. We've all seen this many times. It's demoralising for everyone, so please do try not to be one of those people. Take the time early on to really consider your own and others' views. Discuss and sign off the final spec before the wheels start turning and the machinery grinds into action.

On the other side of town, the pitch team are getting excited. If the company is well organised it will be clear at the start who should be involved at their end. Matching experience and track record to maximise the chances of a win. Unfortunately, I've witnessed internal fighting over who has the "right" to take part. Occasionally the best team isn't put forward because seniority and egos get in the way, or it's someone's turn to perform. This is not helpful. You really don't need a pitch for the pitch.

Setting aside the pitfalls described so far, we'll proceed assuming the company spec/RFP are mostly up to scratch. Information has been exchanged, a timetable has been set so what next?

At this point we should ask ourselves why it is some companies are so much better at winning business than others. How can the ratio of wins to losses be improved? What's *The Monday Revolution* way to improve?

As part of my work I'm often the guy who follows up after a bruising defeat, to discuss with the company who set the brief, what went wrong. And the answers, of course, depend on the circumstances and issues unique to each situation.

But there are common themes that everyone can work on to improve the odds. Companies that recognise the right approach have a much greater chance of success. Let's take a real example of two companies pitching for the account of a multinational food business. To preserve confidentiality and the embarrassment of the loser we'll call one company Green and one Red.

Company Green had an established reputation, several clients of similar size and a good relationship with the chairman. Lately, its win ratio had dropped off to one in four, which the company mainly put down to bad luck and its aggressive pricing policy.

Red had only been in business a couple of years and would be the underdog. With no existing relationship with the company and only a handful of clients to point to, they were going to need to work hard to improve their chances.

As part of the process the company decided to run a series of "chemistry" meetings. These have become common practice in recent years as a way of trying to ensure the right appointment is made. An early look at a potential supplier in a more relaxed setting can work for both sides.

The dates went in the diary. They would be run by the gatekeeper who was in charge of managing the process. Although important, he wouldn't make the final decision. That would be down to the new CEO.

Company Green had been to many chemistry meetings and treated them as a "get to know you moment". An opportunity to informally discuss their credentials and talk about the work they did for others. A time to reinforce why their track record and experience would make them the obvious choice on the day.

Red had a different approach. They viewed chemistry meetings as a vital opportunity to get the inside track. Their pitch team reviewed the brief and thinking to date. They drew up a list of key questions to ask on the day. They wanted to test their approach in the meeting. Importantly, they needed to know the thinking of the new chief executive. Many of their questions would focus on what the decision makers would be looking for specifically at the formal pitch.

The chief executive was new and it was his first role in running a multinational organisation. Red suggested to the gatekeeper that a short call with the CEO would ensure that the time at the pitch would be best spent. Now, they're called gatekeepers for a reason and in some instances, this would certainly be knocked back. However, if carefully presented it can be done. The gatekeeper presented it as his idea to the CEO and the call with Red took place.

Green were all set on the day of the pitch. It was a very important client to win and they'd pulled out all the stops. They'd called the chairman who'd agreed to put a good word in. With clever graphics and props, the whole team was there, each having a role to play. The Green managing partner would do the introductions and summary, but this would be about the experienced squad. He made it clear he wouldn't need to be around on a regular basis. They came away feeling pleased. There hadn't been time for too many questions, but they felt confident their experience and track record would secure the business.

Red took a different approach. Armed with inside knowledge, they'd geared their presentation to the issues the company had identified as the most important. They didn't waste time on lengthy credentials. They provided short punchy charts to support their recommendations. They left sufficient time for a discussion knowing that this would be the opportunity for the company to reveal its thinking. And their opportunity to win the business.

It didn't take the company long to decide to appoint Red. The new chief executive was aware he would need high-level support due to his own inexperience. Green had specifically not offered this whereas Red, following their call, had confirmed their own managing partner would be available as required.

Green were understandably upset. In their eyes, in spite of everything, they'd lost to a company that hardly qualified as a competitor.

Red, of course, understood the importance of when to ask the right questions and being seen to respond. Red's win record for the year was four out five. Green's continued to languish at one in four. They still don't know why.

This story is typical of how some companies so often spend considerable effort hunting down a prospect only to blow it at the final moment. And it's entirely avoidable. Taking the time to really understand what the decision makers in the meeting are going to find important is so critical.

Too often, companies present their credentials as the opening slides. To me that's a show of arrogance: "look at us aren't we great". I always tell pitching companies not to show me anything I can see on their website. Under no circumstances more than ten slides and if they must provide more, put them in the appendix, if that makes them feel better. Sounds harsh, but in a pitch I really want to see what they're made of, not view a well-rehearsed glossy façade that's probably far removed from reality. I want them to ask me upfront how much time is available, get me to confirm what's important and how a decision will be made.

When I conduct my post-mortems for losing pitch teams I try to get to the real reasons for losing. Rarely is it as close as the company makes out. Price is virtually never a factor, just a convenient way of avoiding the true reasons which might be less palatable to the loser.

Put in the positive, teams win because of several common factors. All of which are readily available for anyone to embrace and will certainly improve the odds several fold.

Never take the brief, spec, RFP, whatever it is at face value. It may not truly represent what the company needs. Maybe they haven't thought it through, maybe they didn't know how to. Use every opportunity to learn more about what they need and get them to agree in advance it's what's required. That way you can respond on the day, saying having discussed your real requirements and priorities here's what we think.

This has a very important extra benefit. You took the trouble to find out. You didn't just dust down the last presentation you gave to someone else. Yours is a bespoke set of answers and recommendations. You are passionate and you cared enough to dig deep into the business. This is how you get things done and absolutely reflects how you will perform when hired.

You arrived knowing how the decision will be made. Your advance research informed you how the company will decide. You are aware of the influencing factors and have geared your pitch accordingly. Armed with off-the-cuff examples to parry their questions, complete with case studies of success you've brought other clients, the business should be yours.

OK. I'm not pretending it's easy to do all this. But so many companies don't know how or just don't bother. I can honestly say I'm pretty sure I've awarded contracts to the least bad! Sounds awful but sometimes you think maybe they're just all like this.

I'm often asked what's the single most common reason for failure to win. Without exception it's chemistry. If I asked you what was meant by that, you'd probably say an inability to get on. A dislike or at the very least no rapport from an early stage. If you've not managed to establish common ground and trust prior to the meeting, it's a very tough call establishing that from a very cold standing start.

When asked for feedback from a losing company, in my role as a leader, I've always tried to be open, clear and constructive in my criticism. Sugar-coating the response is no help to them. On many occasions I've said the individuals presented weren't the right people for us. We simply couldn't imagine working with them in the years ahead.

I hear too many tales of pitches made at the end of a long day to executives who've already heard enough. No one gains in these situations so avoid if you possibly can.

On a final note, I recall interviewing a chief executive who had awarded the account to a competitor of the company I worked for as a non-executive director. After a good 20 minutes on a call I was pretty sure I hadn't got to the bottom of the issue as to why we'd failed. Again, it came down to advance information. The company in question was owned by a private equity business who wanted to sell their shares. As they were the owners, we'd concentrated all our efforts on our proposal to find them a trade buyer, as they'd requested.

The chief executive I was talking with acknowledged this was supposed to be the process. But the winning team "had bothered" to leave London and meet the management 200 miles away, at their factory, to hear their priorities. The management didn't want to be sold to a similar bigger business. They wanted to have a new private equity company buy the shares to keep rapid investment coming into the business. At the pitch we lost because we only offered one option and to quote the company, we hadn't bothered with the people who were running the business. Lesson learnt.

The Monday Revolution (you can start on Monday)

1. The prize isn't making the shortlist. It's winning the business. Put at least as much effort into the second as the first.
2. Forward intelligence is critical in gaining advantage. If you know facts your competitors don't, that's a significant result. It's how battles and wars are won.
3. Build early relationships and understand their decision-making process before the day of the pitch.
4. Rehearse roles and anticipate questions.

Chapter 13
Cross-selling

Theory to practice without losing your temper

I'm struggling to know where to start with this. Only because I feel I've so much to say about this simple subject. On paper it's an easy win. We have a sales and marketing team in the field. A blue-chip customer base who are already in the market for additional products. We just need to package them up in the right way with what we're already selling and hey presto – more sales!

I had lunch with the partner of a global professional services company some time ago. We'd met some years before when her company had pitched for our account and lost. We'd had an honest discussion, and both learnt useful lessons about the imprecise process of tendering out business.

Now I was acting as an advisor to several different companies and the partner asked if I could possibly help her solve what had become a difficult problem. She explained that the company had decided to start a new division and had made a considerable investment.

Unfortunately, it wasn't going to plan and could I get involved and fix it? I am quite susceptible to taking on projects without always thinking them through. And this turned out to be a prime example. Two years later, I was still there wondering why I was crammed into a carriage on a Northern Line train in central London, travelling to something I didn't much enjoy.

But I was committed to help, so of course I soldiered on. In the beginning a very experienced and expensive executive partner had been hired. It had taken two years to identify him and persuade him to leave his current job and move with his family from Australia. My friend explained the advisory service he was building was very much demanded by their current clients and it should be a simple matter to convert them from their incumbent supplier to us. They were only using someone else because we couldn't currently service their needs.

Well, after some further meetings, I agreed to help. Truth was, I was quite flattered to be thought of as someone who could solve the problem. The company rarely employed outside its own. "We mostly believe we can solve our own issues," I was told.

It didn't take long to establish why the plan was short on delivering the original expectation. As ever, it's down to the people. But in this case the person. What I didn't appreciate was that companies such as these assume if you've reached a certain level elsewhere, they really don't need to dig too deep into your abilities.

Indeed, it would be improper. If you're a graduate fortunate enough to make the recruitment process, it's tantamount to joining the secret service. No stone unturned. But at partner level, limited evidence is all that's required. Our friend from Australia had joined, been given a budget, agreed a business plan, hired some staff and been left to get on with it.

That is, until he appeared on a spreadsheet somewhere in finance highlighting that his costs and revenue were out of sorts with each other. How could this be? The company has thousands of clients and many would be willing to consider the shiny new service presented by the new Australian leader and his experienced team. Why no sales?

Naively, I had assumed that a company such as this would have in place plans and processes to sell clients additional services. Surely, there would be sophisticated cross-selling incentives on all sides to oil the wheels and provide targets and executive accountability. Surely? But no such thing. I was told subsequently it existed in other parts of the organisation, but not where I was working, sadly.

If you were a partner running an account and had a close relationship with the decision-making client, there was absolutely no reason to share that with a colleague. Indeed, some of the budget might get diverted costing you revenue and personal profit share. Not to mention your contact wasn't necessarily the right person to listen to the new offering. That would be his or her opposite number and the added complication of having to get him/her to introduce your colleague – who you didn't really know and didn't much like from what you'd seen so far.

Notwithstanding all this the company was quite happy with its current supplier and unless we could offer something better at a lower price had no great reason to change.

This is what I'd walked into and the problems didn't stop there. As I said earlier, most companies like to try to solve their own problems. It's cheaper than paying someone else. But occasionally it's just too difficult, so an outsider is summoned. Inevitably, you get the individual who's impossible to turn around, so sometimes the only recommendation you can make is dismissal.

In this particular case he resigned, a good decision all round but it had proved to be a costly mistake. Yet it could have been a great success. On paper and in reality, it should have been the beginning of a new business division. It still could be. What could the company do to make this work?

They could test the new division's offer on some trusted clients. Present them with a prototype, a beta, and say: "If we were to make this would you buy it?" I know companies that always do this and it works. They don't fall into the trap of thinking they always know what their customers want – they ask them.

I was taught as a trainee salesman to always offer customers the opportunity to buy. Of course, you must form a view of their likely reaction and be able to deal with any objections. But to not present the product, giving them the right to buy or refuse, is inexcusable.

So how do you make cross-selling succeed? How could the company I worked for have leveraged their significant global customer base to sell additional products and services?

It requires a cultural shift and a redefined commercial outlook. Coupled with personal financial reward and account-ability across the organisation. No easy task. But to just expect your executives to sell something because it happens to be in the company's interest is hardly a compelling strategy is it?

As ever it starts with the customer. Often a company will be making and marketing complementary products but selling them in isolation. At the buying end there will be different purchasers with differing needs.

I worked with a company that was just starting out in the USA. Having built a successful start-up business in the UK, they were invited to share some office space with a much larger company on the basis this organisation could help accelerate sales by using their sales and marketing team. They took the product of my company but failed to make much headway. Their existing buyers were not really our customers, so they had to make introductions to their colleagues. Their sales guys didn't really know the product and selling it wasn't a matter of life and death. After all, they were accountable and paid for selling the core business, not what they saw as a nice-to-have fringe activity.

Successful cross-selling requires a new market strategy. Our customers are already buying grass seed, can't we sell them a lawn mower and maybe our maintenance services? Of course. But this will require a careful plan and some evidence to establish demand. Why would they switch from an existing supplier? Why is our product superior? What are the benefits? All these questions need to be answered before the sales team are trained, incentivised and accountable. Selling existing services as a bolt-on rarely cuts it. You need to create a culture of importance throughout the company. Not a nice-to-have.

Banks must spend hours of frustration trying to work out how to sell their loss-making current account holders' profitable products. But they rarely provide best in class so why would we buy? Too many companies start in the wrong place. That place being what's in it for them, not what's in it for us.

Another company I know, flush with cash from a very successful year, already provided three ancillary services in addition to its main offer. These extra services enabled it to respond to customers to keep the relationship close and additionally assist in winning new clients. Prudently, the company accounted for them on a separate P&L basis and all were loss making. One of these was a creative business enabling the company to supply clients with design work.

In my view this wasn't a must-have. The market is over-supplied, from large organisations to freelancers. But to my dismay the company had decided scale mattered and had embarked on a strategy to buy a much larger version of what they already owned. When compared with their high-margin retained income business this was not a good idea.

The metrics didn't stack up in my view. Having worked with a few similar creative businesses I'd never invest in one again (I did once and lost my money). Little repeat business, always needing new technical equipment and low margins, due to an over-supplied and consequently highly competitive market. Why exchange your high-quality earnings for a financial profile that will devalue your business?

I'm not sure how the board arrived at the point where they thought this was a good idea. Luckily, I managed to convince them they should invest elsewhere, if at all. Sometimes money is best left in the bank and distributed as a dividend, if it can't be reinvested by the organisation to build further value.

Cross-selling, as we've seen, can take us on a journey into all parts of an organisation and expose weaknesses and strengths, once you start digging around. Everything from taking a very considered approach, selling extra services to providing the evidence for a disposal or close down.

Cross-selling is a prime example of something that should work in theory, providing extra revenue from existing clients at a lower acquisition cost. With sales and account management in place, the synergies and subsequent upside are obvious.

The reality is somewhat different. What it requires is customer insight and complete alignment on your part to make it successful. Companies that understand this are rare, but those that do grow far more quickly than those that don't.

The Monday Revolution (you can start on Monday)

1. Before you embark on any sort of cross-selling initiative, whether an acquisition or bolting on products or services, establish evidence of demand.
2. Look at existing buying profiles. Would your current customer contact be the right buyer?
3. If your executive falls short on product knowledge and the recipient is the wrong person, requiring new introductions on both sides, it's going to be longer and harder than you first thought.
4. Construct a plan that recognises all the hurdles. From buyer demand (what problem are we solving for the customer?) to your own sales executives and process.
5. Set target accountability and reward your executives.

Chapter 14
It's showtime!

High-impact seminars and events

I've attended many events over the years, with mixed results. Some have been exceptionally good, but a number less so. What is it that makes the expense and time spent worthwhile? And how can you ensure that your own event provides lasting value for you and your attendees?

Many companies use events as a business development tool. It allows them to showcase their company's credentials and present their executives in a positive environment they can control. For others the simple aim is profit. Publishing companies who have developed new conference revenue streams to combat falling circulations. Or events companies themselves, by choosing topical subjects and hiring knowledgeable, high-profile speakers, to draw in the crowds.

Whatever the motivation, all should want to stage something successful that can be measured and repeated. There are many pitfalls to avoid and simple steps to take to improve the odds.

Here's *The Monday Revolution* take on running a great event.

First, it's not about what you want to say but about what the crowd want to hear. I remember at a concert when Elton John announced he was about to play his new album in total.

The guy next to me said: "Oh god, it's a double." It's a mistake to start with your own agenda. The leading question should be how do we want them to feel as they leave the room? How can we influence their future behaviour? The simple answer might be that they are more knowledgeable than when they arrived, found it a worthwhile use of their time and have the belief that the company who staged the event are experts in their field.

A common subject approach might be to take an imminent change in the market and be the organisation that owns the expertise and view. I worked with a company that were excellent at this. They timetabled coming legislative changes in a given market and decided they should always do two things. Present the new information as clearly as possible and overlay their expert view on the implications for current and prospective clients.

This required involving recognised experts from their own company, others outside, and building a programme that was compelling in its content. The company knew the recipient of the invitation should instantly feel it was worth checking their personal availability because it would be in their interest to attend.

Prior to the day the company would send out short teasers of information to build expectation. The events were always in the morning and never more than three hours. Why? Well, as we know, attendance falls dramatically after lunch as other priorities take precedence and people head back to the office. And maintaining quality for an entire day can be challenging. So why do it?

The company ensured that each presentation was 15 minutes max and had one clear message. Ten minutes would be given over to Q&A and this would be the real opportunity to provide insight and expertise. Most people don't rehearse this part, but I think it's essential. Not only to anticipate questions and provide an insightful reply, but to use the response as another moment to get a message across. Some politicians do this constantly, unfortunately in a way so obvious it's irritating. Done subtly, it's highly effective.

Having an experienced conference chairman to keep everything tight and on track is essential. Whatever the aim of the event, it's critical to remember that the really important opportunities will occur in the following hours and days. There should be time for networking before and after as people really do value the opportunity to connect with others in their sphere.

Where many companies slip up is putting all the effort into the event itself. To an extent, that's understandable but if the aim is to promote your company, build some new relationships and sell some services or products the follow-up is critical. Yet so many companies don't do this; they wait for the "phone to ring" and mostly it doesn't.

At events I've been involved in I tell the attendees I will personally be in touch to fix a time to meet. I follow this up within 24 hours and it's highly effective. Under no circumstances allow this opportunity to pass. A compelling event invitation on a topical subject, sent in good time to the right people can pay dividends. It will build your reputation and result in new relationships that will generate future profits.

Planning these events is hard work but the payoff can be immense. We are trying to build our business with new and loyal longstanding customers. We need great products and service resources to achieve that goal, and this is the opportunity to showcase to existing customers and introduce new ones to your company.

By presenting your expertise and generously sharing it (for nothing) you can create great momentum. It works at every level, from networking opportunities for you and your current and future clients to creating great material for podcasts, blogs, online streaming and PR.

The Monday Revolution (you can start on Monday)

1. What's coming up? What's topical? What would you like to be known for? Create a rolling document of ideas.

2. Plan. How does point 1. resonate with your current and future customers? It works for you, but will it play to their needs? Revisit assumptions.

3. Plan a year of events and ensure all the associated marketing material goes out on time. Too many times invitations are late or last minute. Usually because too many people have to sign them off. Don't get trapped.

4. Contact the invitees along the way with speaker updates. Build expectation.

5. Discipline your speakers on charts, messages, timing and Q&A. Under no circumstances give them an open brief and leave them to it.

6. Create pre and post networking time.

7. Follow up every attendee, person you networked and those that didn't turn up. Without fail. NOT DOING

THIS IS THE SINGLE LARGEST REASON YOU WILL MISS OPPORTUNITIES.

8. Plan the follow-up as part of the event. Tell everyone there you're going to be in touch to discuss their own particular needs relating to the subject.

Chapter 15
Getting to know you
How to look even more attractive

Prospecting for business can be a time-consuming, occasionally onerous, task. And in spite of new technology, AI and algorithms, it still provides many challenges. But time focused in the right way can be productive and ultimately commercially rewarding.

Customers. We know what they do and where they are. Their habits are transparently available, and we can use a variety of tools to see their behaviour and profile their spending patterns. Furthermore, there is an abundance of software to track our efforts to secure their business. Entire industries exist to support our marketing and sales initiatives.

This is all good and a step change from how businesses used to build a prospect list and customer base. Although robots are taking over many mundane tasks, you can't yet send one to a meeting on your behalf. You might get driven there in a driverless car, but there are no avatars yet capable of representing your company. But this is changing rapidly. Computers already do business with each other, without requiring human intervention.

But for the moment it's down to you to generate interest with people you've often never laid eyes on. I'm regularly asked what's the best way to make contact? "My emails don't get replied to and my voicemail calls are never returned" is a common cry. On the one hand you can contact people directly, but on the other they just don't respond.

We all receive unwanted invitations, usually of a generic nature, and we've long suspended our initial polite demeanour to reply. There are far better ways to connect to people, but they require more effort than just banging out an ill-thought-through email. But I have witnessed people winning large long-term contracts from an initial cold contact. So, it can be done, but what's the secret?

Sometimes it takes a highly personalised email, reflecting the trouble that's been taken to understand the company, its strategy and how you might help. This requires desktop research and respectful confidence. By that I mean assertive without being cocky. The email will offer to share thoughts and knowledge about the sector and perhaps some unique market insight, specially commissioned and unavailable elsewhere. The correspondence recognises you are probably very satisfied with your current supplier; however, other views can sometimes be helpful.

As previously described, when I was tasked with arranging meetings with marketing people at large companies such as Unilever and Nestlé I found the most successful tactic was to have some research on their market that they didn't already have. I concentrated on the grocery sector and could provide data on which FMCG sectors sold best where, by marketing region. This information was specially commissioned by my company for the specific purpose of opening doors and winning advertising spend for the TV company I worked for. I have to say it worked pretty well. And once face to face I could concentrate on the real job in hand. Prising open their marketing wallet and getting some spend.

These two methods are relevant today and both rely on the scarcity factor. If I have something that will make you more successful in your quest for more sales and profits, you're going to be interested. If the price is an introductory meeting it just might be worth paying.

Another common method is LinkedIn. I don't know about you, but I probably receive more initial contacts through this medium than any other. My personal thinking is if you've said yes to a link up, you're saying it's fine to get in touch. But interestingly most of my contacts never have. I guess LinkedIn make it so easy to connect that we all just click the yes button, add to our 500+ connections and don't give it a second thought. But where I have contacted people and requested a call, or a response to something I'll send them, they usually are fine about it and react positively. I would go as far as to say I'm pretty confident I could build out my consultancy practice simply by using my LinkedIn contacts and nothing else.

To get a response it has to be specific. Generic emails just won't do it so don't send them, as it's a waste of your time and does nothing to promote the image of your company. I'm often asked about calls and voicemails. Most people don't respond to uninvited calls and never return voicemails to someone they don't know. Following up with someone by phone is fine if you know them. If you don't, don't bother.

There are plenty of more effective ways of building a network of prospects and we'll cover that now in the next section.

The Monday Revolution (you can start on Monday)

1. Most people find network building very challenging. The fear of rejection looms large. This is an opportunity for those who know what to do.
2. Set quality time aside to plan your approach. There is a big prize at stake and you need to prepare.
3. There are plenty of tools available to build databases and client lists. It is relatively simple to create a network through LinkedIn and many other places.
4. Contact should be well researched, relevant and compelling. Exclusive bespoke information or analysis usually does it and it doesn't have to be lengthy or expensive.
5. Generate curiosity and interest for the recipient.
6. Generic emails, calls and voicemails are a waste of time. Avoid.

Chapter 16
It could be love
Relationships that count for something

There is nothing more important than relationships. They come in infinite shapes, colours and sizes. No two are ever the same. But whether business, pleasure or all points in between, they are without doubt the key to getting things done.

As this is a business book, we'll focus on relationships that have a commercial angle and bypass any other sort. Although recognising there is blurring, confusion and overlap on occasion.

I asked Jonny, who is the best sales guy I know, what has been his most effective way of securing great customers. After all, he's tried just about everything. Yes, everything. He's built an operation for his company in New York from scratch. Yet he'd never even been to the city and soon discovered his bargain basement room in Harlem came at a price. He's now in Brooklyn. Other than this early mishap he's hardly put a foot wrong.

So back to the question: "Jonny, in all your experience what's the most effective way of meeting decision makers, building a network and winning business?" No hesitation whatsoever. "Referrals and introductions. That's it. Focus on who you know and who they know."

"But when you came to NYC you'd never been here before – you didn't know anyone."

Jonny put me straight on that: "You always know someone to get you started. People in the UK made some introductions. Of course, they were mostly not the right people, but they could introduce me to people who knew people. And they did."

You see, when someone makes a personal introduction it's nearly always well received. "Hey David, I'd like to introduce you to Jonny. He's doing some very interesting things in your world and it could be just what your company should be exploring." Or even better: "We use their products and it's made a real commercial impact; you guys should meet up."

Meeting people at conferences, lunches, dinners, speaker events is such an effective way of making contact and building your network. To be successful, it should be approached in a methodical way with some targets in mind. If you just turn up and hope to get lucky, you might. But why not stack the odds in your favour?

Think about who you want to meet, what you can say that they'll find interesting and seek them out. In recent times much of my work has been generated like this and as a consequence, introductions to others have followed. Once I've proved myself as a "trusted advisor", as we like to say (probably a little too often), my existing client contacts offer introductions without a second thought. And I do the same.

As I say regularly to people I meet, who comment on my considerable network and wonder how it came about: "It wasn't an accident." To build a network you've got to be genuinely interested in people. What they do, why they do it and what motivates them. Curiosity is the key. If you're mostly interested in trying to impress, and let's face it we know plenty of those kinds of people, you'll not get very far.

Vince Power, the music business entrepreneur, has introduced me to many people over the years. Vince knows a lot
about relationships and how to involve people he knows and
trusts in his business ventures. He has the charm Irish people
are renowned for and on occasion I've set aside my natural
cautiousness and fallen under the spell. It's not always ended
well but it's never, ever dull. In Vince's world, colourful charac-
ters abound.

Some years ago, Vince introduced me to his friend James.
Another charming Irish guy, in his seventies, with a very cool,
silver-grey ponytail. We had a few drinks and talked about
friendships. James gave me two sayings that he said he often
thought about. "If a man doesn't make new friends in life,
he will end up alone" and "A man's friendships should be in
constant repair".

These two quotes eloquently capture the essence of making
and keeping relationships. Relationships don't just happen; you
have to seek them out, put yourself in a position to be interested, curious, attentive and build rapport and trust.

And once you've done that, relationships need to be developed, maintained and looked after.

People who admire other people's networks can be uncertain how to build their own. Often lacking confidence and
experience, they assume they are built on chance. This of course
does happen but what can you do to improve the chances?
How do you create the circumstances to improve the prospect
of meeting new people who will become business customers,
introducers of others, friends or hopefully all three?

Having the right mindset is important. I liken it to buying
tickets to seeing a gig on a Monday night in an out-of-the-way

location. When it comes to it, you're tired, it's been a long day, the weather is crap and the thought of trekking across town has lost its appeal. But you've got to be there because others are expecting you and being a last-minute let-down isn't your thing.

And guess what? The band are great, much better than expected and you're really pleased you didn't opt out. It's the same with any event; if you don't go, you'll never know what opportunities you missed. So not going can be the easy, but wrong, decision. I'm certainly guilty of this and most of you will be too. Yet we can all cite many examples of showing up and meeting someone that could make it a life-changing experience. Put aside those negative thoughts and step out.

If you want to build a business and create new opportunities, you must be proactive. Meeting people in a seemingly random way can lead to new employees, employers, product ideas, business pitches. In fact, an endless list of interesting and worthwhile situations that can be developed into something meaningful.

Remember, you rarely meet anyone in the office, workspace or wherever you're based doing your work. I remember working at a company where the founder really hadn't thought this through as well as he might. He decided to create in-house a high-class catering facility to entertain current and future clients.

First, however you want to describe it, an office environment is just that. Sure, a different floor with wonderful catering and original artwork helps. But at the end of the day there's little buzz, excitement or cache attached to the in-house lunch or dinner. I was challenged as to why, as a director, I mostly chose not to use the facility, preferring to entertain away from the building.

As I said when asked: "It's all very nice but you don't meet anybody." What I meant was in the outside world I'd bump into people, get introduced to others and maintain my network by being in the right places. However you dress it up in-house, it is, well, in-house and of limited value in my view. Many years ago, I had another boss who insisted we use the company dining rooms. This meant leading guests through the staff canteen to a side room where the food and service fell a long way short. Particularly as most of our guests were used to eating in high-end restaurants.

Again, the message resonates. Planning activity to generate opportunities cannot be over-emphasised. Make time for it. Ensure your week is organised and prioritised to make new acquaintances. I'm not sure where the evidence is that says you're only ever separated by seven people, but work on the basis it's true. Meaning you're never too far away from that all-important contact.

The Monday Revolution values time invested wisely. Building relationships is a great example of how to achieve this aim.

I've already said that my business contacts often came from occasions that were to some extent unplanned. I've built lasting and lucrative business relationships from social events, probably more than any other way. People are more relaxed and willing to share in a way they really never would be by email or call.

By being interested, curious and understanding, people will share their business problems, challenges and plans. And as a result, great things can happen for both sides. Of course, there will be many occasions where it just doesn't work. But perseverance will reward and you will strike gold, which can literally change your life.

In my book this is the hardest bit because it requires proactivity, self-belief and planning. With, of course, the required immediate follow-up. "I'll be in touch tomorrow to fix the meeting" – not "give me a shout if you're interested", because, mostly, no one ever does.

Having built a network of important contacts, how do you ensure they stay interested, relevant and available? This power group can purchase your products, spend more every year, take you to their new company when they leave and introduce you to significant new contacts in their network. As my friend James said, friendships need to be constantly repaired. Not perhaps in the literal sense. But they do need to be maintained and looked after.

Like me you are probably constantly amazed at how useless most organisations are at looking after you, having done the hard yards. In that, they know who you are and that you bought something from them. It can be a tricky old area to be sure. But so often companies are incompetent, at a really basic level.

My local opticians determined, following my eye test with them, that I needed new lenses. The perfect sales opportunity. They had all the information and should have made a sale. But I brushed them off saying I was in a hurry. There was so much they could have done to incentivise me there and then, or later to come back. They hold all the proprietary information. But nothing, no contact, no inducements; they just let me walk away and I've heard nothing since. Crazy.

This is symptomatic of many areas of business. The client is won, the initial pitch was successful, and everyone rejoices in the acquisition of a new customer. But at a future point things start to unravel. The whole process was explained to me in a way that makes a lot of sense, by a business consultant called Eddie I met many years ago. He said:

> "The thing is, business relationships can be compared to personal relationships. Often the same or similar. As that's what they really are, and it makes perfect sense, if you think about them in this way."

When you first meet someone you like, the relationship can develop into one of friendship, trust and mutual respect. Time in each other's company is a pleasure and something to look forward to. Events develop to a contractual relationship or engagement and marriage. And for a while all is fine. But then the sparkle fades. Everything is much more predictable, and the original excitement is in the past. If nothing is done to reignite or rejuvenate then things could be heading for the rocks.

Your partner starts to notice others and they're more interesting and exciting than you. They seem to be able to bring new ideas, answers to problems and are enthusiastic for their company. In the meantime, your original relationship is languishing, with no sign of recovery. It's only a matter of time before cracks start to appear. Sometimes separation and divorce. Often after covertly trying out new partners, who are far more engaging than your current deal.

Eddie explained that it doesn't have to be that way. But often people just become complacent, lazy and don't repair the relationship. In some industries companies are judged on their new client wins. That's how they reward their people so that's where they spend their time. Often neglecting the clients they won previously, who are not feeling particularly loved.

There's a very good fishing metaphor here. When fishing for trout you cast upstream and the fly floats back towards you. It's important you recover the line in the current so there's always a direct communication between you and the fly. If you don't "repair" the line when a fish bites, you'll not be able to strike the hook into its mouth because your line will be lying in untidy loops on the water. The fish will spit the hook out and end up on someone else's rod and line. And that's what happens in relationships. You need to be constantly in touch.

So what to do? Eddie had a strategy not only for client retention but also increasing revenue. "Far easier David, to get existing clients to spend more than new ones." And of course, he's right. If you go about it properly. But first he explained how he tries to ensure his clients don't leave. "It's about exit barriers. It's what a client will lose beyond the central service you provide." And making sure they know that.

Of course, what you provide will depend on what business you're in. Everything from theatre evenings to bespoke reports and information. Regular personal contact to ensure everything is on track. Networking events and introductions. Partner entertainment. Updates on the latest market information to help your contact stay on top. Profiling each client to know their business needs and personal preferences is one of the most worthwhile things you can do. That knowledge allows you to build a set of bespoke exit barriers.

Customer churn is an important performance metric as it's indicative of many underlying issues, good and bad. In many instances, clients don't want to dispense with your services, but you've made it hard for them to stay. Without doubt this is almost always to do with communication (lack of) and neglect. And when the new guys show up brimming with enthusiasm and new ideas... well, it's just hard to say no. Putting the effort into existing relationships is so beneficial, as we've just discussed. It may not be as exciting as the thrill of the chase, but these are not mutually exclusive.

The Monday Revolution (you can start on Monday)

1. Relationships are the most important, precious thing you have in life. Look at what you have already and what you can do to strengthen and maintain your relationships.
2. New relationships occur for all sorts of reasons in all sorts of places. Improve your network by getting out more and being sincerely interested and curious in other people.
3. Be generous in helping other people without always looking at it as a reciprocal arrangement. Good things will follow. You reap what you sow.

Chapter 17
Sorry, I'm in a meeting
Spending time doing the right stuff

A s a basic principle of achieving *The Monday Revolution* way of doing things, your default should be to avoid as many internal meetings as possible. Of the many reasons I hear from people who complain they don't have enough space to get their day jobs done, spending time in meetings is by far the most frequent problem.

Why would this be? Surely the people who organise and run these meetings are the same people that complain. And probably still do. Yet there's something in our DNA that seems to default very quickly to organising a gathering. Whether one to one or a larger group, meetings appear every day and clog up time in a way nothing else can. Some executives have even told me that at the start of the year literally hundreds of meetings are automatically scheduled in their calendar.

This is a crazy state of affairs. Yet the meeting culture, in spite of available technology, instant reporting, slick messaging and data sharing, still pervades our working lives. And it needs to stop. At least it does if you want to build a fast-growing business ensuring every precious minute isn't squandered away discussing some irrelevant side issue.

Did you ever meet anybody who complained that they're not spending enough time in meetings? "I'm sorry, but I've only

23 internal meetings this week and frankly it should be a lot more." Do you notice the people who always seem to be in meetings? They are never available for a call, don't respond quickly to questions and seem to take forever to get things done. Often for these people, meetings are a combination of status "look where I'm going" and insecurity "I need to be in that meeting".

As a business leader I was privileged to control my own diary, at least to some extent. The corporate calendar used to get in the way, but as far as internal meetings were concerned, I could choose. I tried really hard to not hijack my colleagues' time by organising meetings. And if invited, I would usually agree only to participate in the concluding discussion and decision, using the discipline of saying "tell me where you've got to and what we can agree to". Usually, I was in and out in 15 minutes. But being CEO awards the privilege of being able to do that; most can't.

The critical resource here is time. Where is your time best spent? How much do you control and how much is controlled by others? And what can you do to manage your own priorities and influence others to review the time they are effectively stealing from colleagues? The problem with time is it has no shelf life. When it's gone, it's gone. Forever.

Spending time getting the right things done is good beyond the completion or progress of important tasks. It promotes immense satisfaction and wellbeing. Providing energy and enthusiasm that extends beyond you to the people around you. This is the antithesis to dull lifeless meetings with people that suck the energy from your body and mind.

That's the backdrop to this chapter. But the question remains: what can you do about it.? How can you escape the tyranny of time-wasting meetings? If you can't escape, how can you make them better? As an organiser what can you do to create highly productive gatherings that people look forward to joining?

This really is at the heart of *The Monday Revolution*. Being able to look in your calendar and seeing the space to get the right things done. Attending great meetings that you'll contribute to and be valued by others. Most of all, meetings that will push you and the organisation forward. Not slow it up and stall its progress.

A few years ago, I was sitting in a meeting which was being led by a new director. I didn't know him well at that point. But it turned out he was a highly accomplished guy who knew how to engage with people.

You know when meetings wander off the point? Of course you do; you've been in those a thousand times. Annoying people that like having a one-to-one conversation with a colleague that has little relevance to anyone else. In those situations, you look to whoever's leading the meeting to get it back on track.

Well, the new guy had taken a lesson from a completely different environment and applied it to his team meetings. In fact, it drove his entire approach to management. It's a simple tool about goals and priorities. You can apply it from now on and I guarantee an instant improvement in productivity.

His name was Ian and he'd been on an around-the-world yacht race. It was one of those deals where they take amateurs and a limited professional crew. He'd rarely sailed but wanted a challenge to escape his comfort zone. On his first day at sea, the skipper held a meeting with the crew. He let the conversation meander and the meeting became unfocused, typical of those I've already described.

He then said these words:

"Why are we here? We're here because we're trying to win a race. From now on, we only discuss things around this table that make the boat go faster. Nothing else matters."

Those simple words were to have a profound effect on the behaviour of the crew. They absolutely reminded everyone why they were on the boat and what was expected at the daily meeting. If what you're about to say doesn't directly contribute to winning, don't say it.

Those four sentences also said much about the skipper. They demonstrated leadership at a very early stage. From then on everyone knew his instructions would be clear and unambiguous. That instilled confidence in an amateur crew looking for reassurance.

Imagine in your own company if you restricted the agenda and discussion to the key drivers of your business. No tangential waffle. Just a focused conversation about the things that really mattered. Then agreeing clear actions and following them through. "In our meetings we only discuss what we need to do to grow market share, nothing else." Imagine changing the purpose of the "marketing strategy" meeting to the "agreeing one thing to grow market share" meeting. Or "patient interface working group" to "reducing patient waiting time from tomorrow".

Having a stated single aim helps everyone focus on what needs to be done. It works because it ensures people think more clearly about what they're about to say and whether their words qualify. It keeps the meeting on track and prevents side issues taking up valuable time.

It's a good example of taking something completely unrelated, like a boat race, and applying it in a business situation. It's such a very simple but less obvious thing to do.

Looking outside the familiar for a solution can be highly productive and provide a useful exercise for executives. This is an essential Monday Revolution guiding principle. If you've a problem that needs solving, find the answer by identifying someone who's already done it. List the key items that you believe are holding the company back and make team members provide potential answers. But only from outside your current market environment. I guarantee they'll enjoy the challenge and, who knows, you might even make your own "boat" go faster.

Here are the practical ideas to improve your available time, make meeting participation more rewarding and productive, and to run your own meetings in a highly effective way.

In my role as an advisor the most frequent executive cry is "I don't have enough time. There aren't enough hours in the day." I understand; I was there too. It points to a lack of control because your time is being prioritised by others, not you. You need to regain control and it really isn't that hard.

I always insist the clients I'm advising attend an early discussion with me to go through their calendar for a three-month period. I have two questions that drive the point home after about two minutes. "What is the purpose of this meeting?" and "Why does it require your presence?" Well, as you might expect, the purpose is often unclear and sometimes unknown, at least to my executive. "Why are you attending a meeting when you don't know what it's for?" "Well, people know when to include me." "Really? Because they can't make a decision without you? Are you one of those managers?"

There are many possibilities here but without exception and too much persuasion, we eliminate or delegate meeting attendance. You can do the same. Ask those questions and free up swathes of time. Then enter in your calendar some fictitious entry to prevent others from hijacking the space with some auto-diary crawler. At a stroke you now have more time.

Greg was summoned by his bosses and told his performance was so impressive he was being invited to join a series of executive committees. Strategy, budgets, remuneration discussions were about to head his way. Greg thought this was a death sentence. Or at worst a living hell. His clever response was he was grateful to be recognised but he wouldn't be any good at that grown-up stuff. His value to the company was simply to continue to do what he did best. Win and develop customer relationships that would endure over many years.

"But Greg, this could lead to greater things. You might become CEO." Greg decided if sitting in long meetings, pouring through reports and spreadsheets was the price of promotion, it really wasn't for him.

It could well be a meeting is unnecessary, at least at the early concept stage of trying to solve a problem or create an opportunity. Try encouraging work to take place away from a room that involves the time of six people getting together. That's around a day of productivity given up. And they'll never get that time back. First question: is a meeting the best way of moving this forward? Consider other options before consigning people to an airless room with paper cups or a hipster breakout space for mint and lemon water.

Conduct an audit of regular meetings in this way. Why are we meeting? What is the purpose? What will be decided? What will we do differently as a result of meeting? How long does it really need to take? Really? Could it be shorter – it probably could?

And then: "Who is responsible for ensuring what we agreed gets done?"

Apply this to every meeting in your calendar and particularly to those you're personally tempted to organise. Done properly with your colleagues, this will result in fewer, shorter meetings, with much better results. Try it.

Build a Monday Revolution culture. Imagine working in a company and being able to say:

> "We don't have many internal meetings. We decided they're mostly a waste of resources. The ones we do have are really focused on one or two key decisions and they never take too long. It's a real joy to attend."

OK, the last point may be pushing reality, but you know what I mean.

If you're a director, there will be those mandatory board meetings requiring the need to plough through the company accounts with the auditors. I can't tell you how quickly my boredom threshold was breached on these occasions. My issue, certainly; not theirs. Mostly they were extremely well run. But if ever there was a need for a rethink, audit meetings would be top of my list. Observing the finance team trading respectful blows with KPMG made me think there must be a better way than this to establish the financial integrity of the company's performance.

In order to get through the time, I resolved to ask a question every ten minutes. Not to look smart but to stay awake by trying to engage in what was essentially a closed meeting, even though I was in the room. If you find yourself in a situation where you have no control over the agenda, timing or your own presence, try it as a last resort.

You'll notice I've focused on the issue of internal meetings. Because external meetings often have a different status in people's minds. More junior people see external meetings as broadening their horizons. It's more grown up to leave the building and meet a customer or supplier. There's status attached to being allowed out to represent your organisation.

I am a proponent of face-to-face meetings, particularly if you need to persuade someone to behave in a certain way. Like buying something of high value, for example. Or to build a long-term relationship, partnership or such like. Digital messaging has its place but it's no substitute for getting together if the circumstances require it.

I say if the circumstances require it because often we meet when we really don't need to get together. I have a few rules about this here which I'll share.

If I don't want to meet because it's very apparent there's nothing in it for me, I don't arrange a meeting. Sounds harsh but saves time for everybody. I'm all for networking but I've found too often there's not been much in it for the person I've met or me either. An initial scheduled phone call is often a better way of determining common ground. "Look, I'm travelling around a lot over the next few weeks, let's fix a call instead of meeting."

I never agree to breakfast, lunch, dinner or drinks with anybody I've never met. Far too time-consuming for what could turn out to be something that could be established in a few minutes or turns out to be a waste of time.

The other side of this coin are those meetings you feel could result in something good happening, but the other person needs convincing. Experience tells you if you can get in front of someone, establish common ground and rapport, you're in with a chance of persuading them to do something. In these instances, the onus is on you to convince them to meet.

The Monday Revolution (you can start on Monday)

1. Avoid arranging internal meetings as a default response.
2. Audit your calendar and ask yourself what the meeting is for and why you need to be there. Do this as a quick-fire exercise and withdraw from as many as you can and time limit your presence at others.
3. Audit company meetings. They'll thank you for it. Why are we meeting? What is the purpose? What will be decided? What will we do differently as a result of meeting? Get useless meetings consigned to history.
4. If you can't escape, engage in the meeting by asking regular questions to prevent boredom and unrelated thoughts. Do not write a shopping list.
5. Build a Monday Revolution culture. "We don't have many internal meetings. We decided they're mostly a waste of time. The ones we do have are really focused

on one or two key decisions and they never take too long. It's a real joy to attend."

6. Don't agree to external meetings just because someone invites you to get together. Validate the purpose first. This will be good for both of you.

7. Face-to-face meetings are critically important to building relationships, establishing trust, rapport and often central to getting things done. Apply judgement in deciding when and what to attend.

Chapter 18
I need help, with my help

Independent advice

No matter the track record or accomplishments, highly experienced business leaders know when to seek independent advice. In fact, they're far more likely to do that than newer recruits. Perhaps because the new guys believe there's some sort of failing attached to not being seen to knowing all the answers.

Help. Yes. But what sort?

A good starting point can be to analyse your own personal strengths and weaknesses. This may be based on self-awareness or perhaps a result of feedback from others. Or a current situation or challenging problem where there doesn't appear to be an obvious in-house remedy.

This need for advice was succinctly put by a very successful guy who had started his own business but was having a few issues and recognised he needed some help. His fast-growing company had become a multimillion-pound organisation, but his systems and processes had, understandably, not kept in step. Rather than make it up, he wanted to know what best practice looked like.

On a recommendation he hired in an experienced advisor to take a look. The resulting work provided him with a number of options on how to upgrade and in some instances fast-track improvements. Some of these he might have got to himself, but not as quickly. Others he didn't know existed. In the main these were basic foundation areas, such as data storage, employment contracts and health and safety requirements. The sort of things that get lost in the heady rush for sales and profits. Every leader should review their "hygiene factors"!

Fortuitously, I was offered a last-minute place as a guest at a charity lunch. That's where I met a divisional managing director who needed help. His problem is commonly encountered by senior people, easily defined and hard to resolve.

As we all know, you can't easily help someone who resists change and is in denial. We all get frustrated with others who refuse to acknowledge their problems or dismiss advice that would solve the issue. Sometimes, we only take action at the moment of crisis and frequently that's too late, the point of no return having already arrived.

My new contact wasn't quite in that terminal situation. He realised his problems needed fixing and quickly. The division was losing money and his job was on the line. This would be his personal point of no return; he could see it coming and that made him very uncomfortable. However, he explained he'd hired some outside help and we discussed how he saw that working out. I wondered how this was going to go and whether anyone could fix the problems. So, he agreed to share progress over the coming weeks.

First, his independent advisor met a number of people who worked above, below and alongside him. The leader was slightly uncomfortable about this; he wanted to be there and hear for himself. But it was explained this would hold people back and there was a real need to get to the bottom of the issues that were causing the problems.

Evidence was collected from many individual perspectives. Often, it's the most junior people that can see what's wrong and how improvements can be made. He needed to know what type of company and people he was dealing with; only then could he share his findings and prepare recommendations.

The remedies to their problems had to be provided in context and the issues became abundantly clear very quickly. Clients were departing, and sales were well down. There was no dispute around this. But the reasons given varied from person to person. Of course, no one said it was down to them personally or they should have tried harder. Some blamed the economy, others the competition. But mostly the organisation.

The advisor soon saw through the excuses and felt ready to explain what was wrong with the division and how it could be fixed. He explained what he'd found and what should be done about it. Remarkably, the decline in the business began originally from a decision that produced unintended consequences. The most successful guy at securing new clients had been promoted and no longer brought in much new business. There had been no replacement.

In the ensuing discussions with management and colleagues there were few answers to the often-asked question: "What are we selling and why should anyone buy it?" Although the division was awash with internal meetings, none addressed how to gain more clients. There was limited thought given to the service they were selling. And many of the senior people refused to take responsibility for bringing in new business.

It was unintentional of course, but the HR and training departments just seemed to add another layer of administration. Annual reviews and bonuses were a matter of management discretion. Underperformance was tolerated and anyway there were no consequences for doing a bad job. Of course, many of these problems were deeply embedded and nothing an outsider said would make a difference. At least not in the short term and let's face it, time was at a premium.

It may not sound like it, but this was in fact mostly good news. Why? Because there was so much wrong it was crystal clear why the business was failing. What was needed was a simple plan to mend the parts that could be fixed in the short term. Particularly the things the director controlled. At this stage, anything that required board-level approval was definitely off-limits.

Our director began to feel better. He could see from the recently acquired evidence that turning things around was not impossible. That evening he told his wife that he felt his job could be saved. He slept better that night, something that hadn't occurred too often lately. And when he woke up, he looked forward to going to work, knowing that with the right help, he could turn things around. *The Monday Revolution* was starting to take shape.

The principal problem was a shortfall in new business. There was no plan to win new clients and although he was the guy in charge, he lacked the skills and experience to know what to do about it. But, having taken a look at the business and having been in similar situations, the advisor had a pretty good idea what was required. Over a period of two years the division turned from an embarrassing failure to the most successful in the company. Here's how they did it.

They fixed a meeting with the partners of the division to explain the extent of the problem. They presented the key financial facts clearly and honestly. Everybody could see that unless something was done, the business would eventually cease to exist. The director said it was a shared responsibility as no one person could fix the problem. Each individual would have an important role to play and become accountable for solving the crisis.

They looked at their products, compared them to the competition and concluded many were not fit for purpose. They had to be far more innovative and compelling. They needed to understand what their potential clients required to solve their own problems. In the past they'd offered what they thought people wanted; now they were going to gather evidence to establish what they needed.

As with many companies, business development gets pushed to one side in the good times. When revenues are increasing and targets are being achieved, why worry too much about the future? Prospecting for new clients is hard and doesn't come naturally to many people. Particularly in service companies where people are hired for their professional skills, not their ability to market themselves and their organisation. In this division that was certainly the case.

At one time there had been a fairly regular meeting when business development would be discussed but that was about all. No clear actions, more an exchange of who knows who. Attendance dwindled as the meeting was, to a great extent, pointless.

Now things needed to change. A fortnightly meeting was scheduled and attendance was compulsory. No excuses; you had to be there. But unlike previous gatherings this one had a clear purpose. Armed with their improved products, designed by asking current and future clients what they really needed, they focused in on one or two particular market categories. They knew if they tried to do everything at once, they would fail. Concentrating on specific areas made the process more manageable. They built a pipeline of prospects and allocated responsibility around the table. Each person had ten companies to contact, fix a meeting and win some business. Every fortnight they would meet and review progress.

Of course, this was not without its problems as you would imagine. In spite of it being a "compulsory meeting", some still attended occasionally. Unsurprisingly, these guys won little new business and were more than happy to leave it to others. It proved tough to meet new potential clients from a standing start.

But over time they began to learn what worked. They developed their own individual techniques, built personal networks and grew in confidence. The director led the meeting and the advisor provided experience and support, using examples of what worked. They role-played contacting clients to anticipate objections and shared their own experiences to help each other. They quickly realised introductions and referrals were a much easier way of getting face-to-face meetings, so concentrated on how they could get to know more people.

At the fortnightly meeting the pipeline grew, priorities were set and accountability ruled the day. It felt uncomfortable turning up without having done what was agreed. Consequently, people took responsibility for their actions, shared their successes and asked for advice when they needed it. And guess what? Gradually they started to win some business. Net losses turned to net gains. But there was one more thing our director was advised he needed to do.

The discretionary appraisal and reward system had to change. A newly designed performance-related model was built, based on how they wanted people to behave. Colleagues were rewarded for their results and promoted on merit. Eventually the division built a culture based on proactivity and shared ownership. And the under-performers, the ones who choose not to get involved? They mostly left or moved elsewhere in the company.

This was very hard work. It took a lot longer than they anticipated and both would have liked. But the decision to seek independent experienced advice paid off. The division became the company's most successful. The director was promoted and is frontrunner to be the next chief executive.

The Monday Revolution (you can start on Monday)

1. Consider using outside independent advice, particularly for deep-seated problems that have remained unsolved for too long.
2. But it isn't about outsourcing the problem. You haven't hired someone else to fix it. It's still your responsibility and you need to be fully engaged.
3. Independent advisors should provide advice within the context of your business. Therefore, they need access to a broad group of individuals to understand the culture and rules of your company.

4. Treat the engagement as a partnership seeking a common goal. A healthy relationship based on candour will triumph but recognise there will be occasional healthy conflict between you, along the way.

Chapter 19
Fast digital

Mandatory transformation.
No exceptions.

In a very small way, I helped a business by providing advice and some investment. It started because a colleague I worked with said: "You should meet Richard, he runs a training company and he's looking for advice." I met with Richard.

He transformed his company from an unscalable classroom-based training business into a global digital organisation. We train international companies from the UK to Australia, often thousands of people in one organisation, all at the same time. We have the best platform and product in the world. So far!

My contribution was minimal. Some views when it mattered and the privilege of being their first investor. Being involved brought home to me the increasing need for every business to get up to speed in the language of digital – before opportunities are missed, the best people don't join, or products become outdated and irrelevant. If your core business is making filing cabinets, it could be time for an urgent rethink.

It's one of the most challenging issues facing every business: unlocking the commercial opportunities that exist when you get your act together with digital. In digitising your operation you'll have immediate direct access to information that for years only existed in handwritten report form, before finally finding its way onto an Excel spreadsheet.

Today, companies are judged by their digital presence. The option of digital no longer remains. What might have been a "nice-to-have" is now required and expected. Demonstrating products and services, transacting, customer service and all forms of marketing require digital skills and knowledge from everyone.

Yet many organisations are still operating in a grey area and haven't fully embraced digital, even though it's how the world now works. These companies need to get up to speed because if they don't respond to customers' expectations, they'll get passed by.

Here's a harsh example of a company that found out the hard way that they'd been left behind. Put simply, they received an invitation to tender for business from a large client in the financial sector. The brief was detailed and required recommendations on the use and impact of digital media. Although the team were experienced professionals, their digital knowledge was limited as their strengths lay in the more traditional way of doing things. Their response to other areas of the brief was pretty spot on but their digital weakness immediately excluded them.

The client said it was very straightforward:

> "We divided the responses into those with apparent digital knowledge and those without; unfortunately, you were in the second pile."

Expectation failure and a loss of opportunity to earn some substantial fees resulted.

How you behave in the digital economy will determine your success or lack of it. If you don't understand what it is you don't know then hire help. And if you don't know what help you need, get help with your help. Yes, it's a minefield and there are countless companies out there waiting to take your money. But don't use that as an excuse for not moving fast enough. *The Monday Revolution* requires immediate digital action.

A business acquaintance of mine joined a new company and was presented with the latest marketing materials. There was a new website and brochure positioning the company as experienced and worthy of further interest. At least I'm sure that's what they intended. But the result was confusing and mostly dull.

On further discussion it transpired that the various divisions of the company couldn't agree. Politics had prevented the right decision being taken and the manager was very old school – "we don't want any online video". The result was built on a series of compromises and was far from compelling. Lack of leadership and client focus will cost this company money, no question.

Companies are judged by their digital presence. If your website, app or any other digital interface are letting you down your bottom line will suffer, be in no doubt. And mostly you'll never know about the opportunities you missed. Those anonymous potential customers silently clicked their way to a competitor. And all you'll be able to do is look at a stats report that tells you that harsh reality.

I recall an interview with a senior person in the medical profession proudly explaining that they "don't do digital". "I like the old fashion methods best." Bringing the older, analogue-established generation into the digital world is a priority.

Problems and opportunities are not just limited to what the world outside can see. As part of your digital review, look at how you store and retrieve data. Many companies who should know better are keeping sensitive information on Excel spreadsheets instead of cloud-based encryption. CRM systems, a critically important client management tool, lie unused, alongside the company intranet which was supposed to transform internal communication.

I know a lot of this stuff is difficult to get right. I've run and worked for companies (still do) who absolutely get the importance but struggle with the execution. I'm not a consultant in this area and have no qualification to offer advice other than my own experience.

My one observation, based on my own mistakes, is one of expecting too much. By that I mean building systems that are too complex for the user to easily grasp and require too much input before they produce anything meaningful.

Designing digital systems that can be built on, as users become confident, is a far more successful strategy. The all-dancing, all-singing show rarely delivers. Think about it this way. Apple update their iPhone operating system and we mostly complain we can't find what we're used to. After a while it becomes the norm. Their very early operating system bears no real resemblance to the current one. As Apple developed it, they took us with it. When buying or building in-house digital tools, do the same.

Organising information and using those insights to drive profitable growth should be a given. Yet too often we fail to make the required investment and realise the opportunity.

We all know that smart companies have robust policies and systems to manage activity. However, applying the same principles to our own organisation appears to defeat many of us.

I was working with a company that illustrated this perfectly. We were talking about how to ensure we kept in touch with past, current and prospective clients. This is a successful company, but its processes and systems haven't kept up and growth was starting to slow. Now turning over many millions, I asked this question of the CEO:

"How are you keeping track?"

"What do you mean?" he replied.

"I mean, you have a lot of people you're talking to and you need to ensure you have a process, otherwise opportunities will be missed. Do you have a CRM system?"

"Yes, yes of course we do."

"Great, may I see it?"

"Why?"

"Because I want to see what's there and how it's helping you keep track."

"Well, it's not really up to date."

"Why?"

"Because we don't really use it; to be honest we all keep our own records."

"OK, can I see yours then?"

"I don't write mine down; it's all in my head."

Does the folly of this need pointing out? Hopefully not. I explained to the busy leader that he was attempting an impossible task and that keeping a live record of client contact, purchasing history, a timetable of future actions and enabling his colleagues to view activity would pay dividends.

Like many executives he was often frustrated with the team's commercial planning but was a leading protagonist of this failure. A business leader was once again setting the wrong example.

Reluctantly he agreed to change his act and ensure the CRM data was current. Only then, I explained, could we have a meaningful discussion about the opportunities this data might offer. After some false starts and resistance from his colleagues, we're starting to get there. There will be a tipping point where it eventually becomes "it's how we do things around here".

Contrast this with a similar fast-growing business where the CEO recognised the opportunity and took a very proactive stance.

"We're generating lots of customer data and I think it's a bit of a goldmine; question is how can we get the most out of it?" We reviewed how the information was managed and how we could organise it in a way that made sense for the business. We concluded that Sales Force (software management tool) was the right system. Significantly, it would integrate with and eventually replace our own inadequate IT platform.

That was only stage one. The company needed to organise the data and produce actionable information reports that would reveal new commercial opportunities. This posed more of a problem, but only for the short term. At stage two we hired a data analyst, familiar with Sales Force, who could provide the required insight.

Stage three required the executive level to act. So, we ensured that customer contact, pricing, trends and a host of other "goldmine" information guided and influenced our everyday activity. And the commercial effect on the company performance was dramatic.

Beware the danger of oversupply. It's so easy to produce reports that if you're not careful you can drown in information. Remember, producing and managing data doesn't achieve anything; in fact, it can be a considerable drag on performance. For example, it can cause people to spend time generating reports for internal meetings whose original purpose has long been forgotten and can be a dangerous eventual consequence. The value lies in interpretation and execution. And value is only ever created if something happens. How many times have you sat in a meeting or presentation and the general response has been "interesting"? What we're looking for is data that makes us sit up, take a sharp intake of breath and set the pulse racing. We're looking for insights and occasionally we will strike gold. That's *The Monday Revolution* approach.

Of course, you'll have your regular reports, measuring your KPIs and that's necessary and fine. Just be careful with how much you produce and make sure you can do something with it.

The Monday Revolution (you can start on Monday)

1. Being a digitally transformed company is now necessary for survival and growth.
2. Accountability at the top level. You're in charge. What do you expect by when?
3. What data are you generating and how is it managed? Who is responsible for interpretation and making recommendations to identify commercial opportunities?
4. What's the digital investment plan? You need to do more than just keep up.

Chapter 20
How did that happen?
Screw-ups and left-field moments

How do you deal with those unexpected left-field moments? An impossible question, you might think. When life is good, business and personal life move harmoniously in sync and it's hard to imagine why this should possibly end. And an analysis of the facts serves to confirm this happy state is likely to continue beyond the horizon. "If it ain't broke, don't fix it" is the well-trodden maxim. As a wise colleague of mine once observed, we don't tend to question why everything is going so well. It's only when things go wrong that we reflect on what we could have done better.

I can remember thinking, after serving up record profits to our investors, that this would potentially never end. Ridiculous of course, but I thought it was logical. Increasing product demand, a quasi-monopoly due to government regulations and operating margins that could only improve as the revenue tumbled unrestricted to the bottom line.

When I announced our first profit warning, I felt slightly different, as you might expect. On reflection I've concluded that it's human nature to look through life's lens and conclude that the current position is likely to continue. When times are good why shouldn't that be?

Yet history confirms that at some point there's likely to be a disruption to this steady state. It might be recoverable, or it might be fatal. We all know we're going to die. What would help would be knowing how and when. In business the outcome is far less predictable. Does any business need to die? You can argue not. If it stays relevant, by adapting to changing circumstances, there's no reason to fail.

Unfortunately, our DNA has an in-built steady state. As we get older, we become far more risk averse. And it's generally older people running businesses over a certain size. Constantly challenging the status quo, planning for the downside, recognising market shifts and emerging competitors does not come naturally to many captains of industry. Many have made more money than they need and the drive and enthusiasm they once had has faded. In my book a safe pair of hands means you can forget about anything important happening to grow the company.

In some instances, there's a gradual erosion of market share and margins. Or perhaps a left-field moment that leaves us wondering how we allowed that to happen on our watch – as discussed elsewhere. Careless, aggressive or crooked accounting is commonly how companies can collapse in a matter of days. This is a regular occurrence. Of course, it's only the big guys that find their way into mainstream media. And as this happens, we stand back in awe unable to comprehend how something that large and established could now lie in ruins in what seems a matter of hours.

I have been on the board of some extremely successful businesses and more than one business that failed. If you stay in a company long enough, you'll be there when something completely unexpected blindsides the organisation. Sometimes hindsight might suggest the reasons were obvious. But that's not always the case. And survival and recovery rest on how equipped you are to deal with it.

Nasty surprises happen. It's an inevitable fact of life. Everything seems to be going well then suddenly something comes out of left field that you weren't expecting. In our personal lives that's a life-threatening illness perhaps, affecting you or someone close by. An unexpected redundancy, a huge loss on a "safe" investment. In business it can be a myriad of things. From the sudden resignation of the chief executive, to an industrial accident, fraud, data theft or a failed supply chain. You don't have to look far; everyone has a story.

We can try to plan to mitigate the effect of the unknown by having some sort of contingency in place. In our personal lives we might buy medical insurance and regularly update our affairs, so others can take over if needed. In business, particularly for companies listed on the stock exchange, a formal approach to risk is required.

I've been part of risk committees where the task has been to anticipate what might go wrong. I think it's fair to say that although it's an important exercise, anticipating chronic failure in a part or all of the business is a pretty difficult and depressing experience. It's also fairly easy to list the obvious but the obvious often isn't what happens.

I recall the time I scheduled a trip to the USA visiting several cities. After some careful planning and fairly tedious online booking procedures, my east coast–west coast arrangements firmed up and I was set to go. Visiting friends and fishing were the highlights of the agenda and timings had finally fallen into place.

Except I never made it. Perhaps I should have anticipated the hazard. But as it only occurs around once or twice in thousands of years, I didn't even know it was a possibility.

I suspect airlines have some of the longest risk registers known to man. Engine failure, on-board fires, terrorist attacks, mentally ill pilots. I can readily recall all of these, although I try not to when at 37,000 feet above the Indian Ocean.

But it was a volcanic ash cloud from Iceland that disrupted the global fleets of the international carriers. And kept me in the UK. Did this possibility feature on their corporate radar? Did the chief risk officer have it in his sights? Maybe. But to a casual, infrequent international traveller like me it wasn't apparent, as the chaos literally rained down.

Contradictory opinions took hold. From how long it would last, to whether planes could actually fly safely through a cloud of volcanic ash without the engines seizing up. In an extreme and bizarre example of leadership, the director of one airline headed into the clouds with just a flight crew to prove all would be fine. It was, I'm afraid, self-serving, desperate and rather unconvincing.

I'm all for senior people leading from the front but this had the appearance of a reckless act, literally flying in the face of many an expert opinion. I wonder when the board reviewed risks to the company it included volcanoes and the director risking his life (and millions of pounds of shareholder value) to try to mitigate the problem. I suspect not.

Of course, it's impossible to second-guess every possible business risk. But if you don't have a plan for the obvious, you'll be on the hook if it happens on your watch. It's at times like these the true colours of the management are revealed. We'd all rather not deal with bad news and senior executives are no exception to this very human trait. Particularly when it involves some face-to-face responsibility with staff, customers and the media.

Of course, some risks are entirely avoidable. If your business chooses to mine for precious stones in a war-torn, politically unstable country that's suffering from a ravaged economy and hyperinflation, you probably know what might go wrong. This is a judgement call of profits versus risk. But most of us won't be joining you; all of those risks exist and might be heading your way, in some shape or form, at some point soon.

My personal experience has been exposure to political decisions that have delivered, for the most part I would say, unintended consequences. Generally negative. Taxation changes that impacted consumer behaviour. Or regulatory changes, such as auctioning off the country's television broadcast licences, which sucked money and resources out of the system and achieved just about nothing for the viewer.

I've also experienced changing sentiment towards companies operating in overseas territories. These often appear as additional charges, changes in employment law or other onerous regulations. Often to appease local businesses who feel they're being squeezed by unwelcome overseas competition (us). Tariffs and import restrictions remain a risk for anyone operating internationally.

I'm writing this book in 2019. I'm hoping it will have a long and healthy shelf life, as will its author. I'm trying to avoid examples that may have lost their relevance by the time you read these words. I was saying earlier about the zen state of how we always think our current circumstances are sustainable. But it just isn't so. Disruption started when our ancestors discovered fire and invented the wheel. And it's continued unfettered ever since. Our capacity for invention and change has no limits. There's no doubt your business will be challenged by someone who thinks they can do what you do. Except do it faster, better and cheaper.

Situations may or may not be within your control. In running a company you're entitled to expect the lights to work when you turn up at work or home. The basic utilities that we all take for granted are backed up by suppliers and we rely on them to take care. And mostly they do. But if there's a failure, you'll be expected to have a contingency plan.

Some areas are just too specialised or custom made for you to risk having no plan B. IT systems are very much in this category. In my book you just have to spend what it takes to develop and protect them. Yet I'm constantly surprised to find so many businesses that take, what I can only assume, calculated risks to remain exposed without the required backups or alternative systems.

Finance has been covered earlier in some detail, but perhaps you need to hear it again? The central message is this. If you're in any sort of role that requires responsibility for spending or receiving money, you have an absolute duty of care and ownership. That goes for whether you're a junior manager or the president of a Fortune 100 business. It's unquestionably your role to understand the finances of the organisation. End of lecture.

I worked with a food business that really did have all their eggs in one basket. Their supply chain relied on a series of well-intended, like-minded, high-quality producers. All was well until one Christmas a fox burrowed their way into the chicken shed and murdered all the chickens. This wasn't a minor incident. The supply chain suffered huge disruption and alternative sources were hard to find at such short notice. The company now has multiple suppliers across most of its popular product ranges. And has extended that principle to other mission-critical parts of the business. Worth considering across every aspect of your business I would suggest.

And what about key people and how much they matter? Organisations are supposed to anticipate executive change and have the replacement ready groomed and waiting patiently in the wings for the next step up. Great theory but I don't think in practice this often works too well.

Companies are required to succession plan but rarely seem to succeed. There are a number of reasons for this. Ambitious people don't want to be hanging around for some replacement moment in an indeterminate timeframe. Not least of all because they're on the receiving end of outside approaches that exist today. An effective executive team involves people with complementary skills so it's unlikely the successor will be a direct replacement with the same qualities. There may be no obvious internal candidate.

When a key person leaves, the company endures a mild state of paralysis, while the leaver works their notice and the replacement works theirs. During this period important decisions are usually on hold awaiting the new person. They usually and understandably need to have a look around, conduct a review and come up with a plan. At least 12 months lost I would say.

When I join or advise a business, I ask simple performance questions. Such as what are your weekly priorities? Who are our most important customers and when did you last meet them? How much cash is in the bank and how long will it last? Sometimes my intrusive nature doesn't make me particularly popular with one or two of my new colleagues. In the spirit of now and *The Monday Revolution*, early decisive action matters. Not hanging around for months putting things off. But it sends a certain message, not always welcomed by some.

The immediate overriding importance is to take public responsibility. When I say public, I mean not hiding from the unfolding drama or delegating to a lesser person, or worse still employing a "spokesperson". When I was in charge, I made a point of always standing in front of as many company people as would fit in our largest room. I would tell them what had happened and why, together with what we were doing about it. Unfortunately, this type of communication, or in some instances any type of communication, is often sadly lacking. Which means everyone not involved fills the void by making assumptions, because without information why wouldn't they?

The company needs to have a plan to mitigate the risks posed by the unknown. This requires process and procedure to immediately take charge and respond to whatever it is that has suddenly appeared to spoil your day. Good managers know that this is a moment to step up and do the right thing. As the manager of a very public business, in every sense of the word, I had my fair share of crises to respond to and take the lead. I've no doubt there were times where the company could have made a better fist of it. But I would challenge anyone to question our immediate honesty and visible intent to do the right thing.

The corporate world is littered with examples of companies that misfired, misstepped and then dealt with the aftermath badly. From Enron to Tesco you couldn't make it up. We stand back incredulous that despite all the checks and balances, boards full of worthy, highly experienced executives, they still manage to preside over some monumental screw-ups.

At *The Monday Revolution*, we are always looking for better ways. Learning from studying the actions of others, by looking outside our own particular world. Applying a particular situation to our business, as if it was real, is a great use of time. Rather than be relieved it hasn't happened to us, why not examine what we would do in similar circumstances?

On your next "away-day" use some of the time to review what's mission critical, the things you really can't do without. And planning your own crisis falls into this category.

As a brief aside, I'm aware that there is an underlying theme to this book. In fact, there are many. One of my many regrets is the time I spent wasted, doing the wrong things. I don't mean bad things; I mean time spent that resulted in nothing much moving forward. Little getting done. *The Monday Revolution* is the antidote to this if applied correctly.

Away-days fall into this category for me. So, if you must have one, do something useful with it. By that I mean don't have an oversubscribed agenda and an endless stream of PowerPoint decks. Use this expensive and valuable time well to challenge what you do and why you do it. There's so much information around from other businesses; every day there's another great case study.

Companies generally review their performance on a quarterly or annual basis. Strategic priorities change, resources are allocated, and budgets are updated. This is usually a fairly benign, steady-as-you-go state of affairs. It's OK but it's not great. Frequently, away-days are part of this process and frankly having wasted too much of my life in airless rooms, they're not for me any more. Often these sessions are dedicated to longer-term thinking, quality time to consider the future. But in reality, nothing much really changes as a result of spending time with your colleagues out of the office. Unless you do something about it.

There are lots of ways a company can review what it does. Here's one way of doing that which is highly effective, doesn't involve PowerPoint and will deliver great benefits.

In order to set the scene, you need to create a sense of crisis. Larger companies often do this by asking their advisors to review their defence strategy, in the event of a hostile bid for their shares. But that's only part of the story. Because it only covers how the company is likely to respond. Rarely does it lead to the company doing anything very specific, other than tightening up a few previously agreed procedures.

Take the audacious Kraft bid for Unilever in 2017. Much has been written about this, but just to remind you of the story. Paul Polman, the Unilever CEO, received an unwelcome call from a company partnered with Warren Buffet (the world's most successful investor of his time) saying they'd like to make a multibillion-dollar offer for the business. After a very short, uncomfortable period, the offer was withdrawn, but life for Mr Polman and his team would never be the same again.

That moment of crisis shone a very bright light on Unilever. The company's track record, performance and strategy were the subject of global discussion in mainstream media and government. According to an independent report, the majority of investment managers holding the stock would have preferred the bid to progress. Why? Because they're judged on the performance of their share portfolios and takeover bids mostly come at a premium price, boosting returns.

But now that's gone away, investors want to know how the share price can be grown in other ways to exceed the bid price. The number the board just turned down. They focused on the underperforming divisions and slow-growing territories, where the company has a large presence. They've drawn attention to Mr Polman's altruistic approach to business, suggesting he should concentrate his efforts on improving commercial performance. Not just saving the planet.

On the face of it, the margins at Kraft were far superior to Unilever's. If nobody had really noticed that before, they did now. The pressure was on to improve performance quickly and be seen to be doing so.

In response, Unilever have announced an accelerated strategic review. The board presented some significant changes, which included a radical review of each division and the contribution it makes. Already the margarine company they owned has been sold.

Here's the key question and it's not just aimed at Mr Polman. Why does it so often take an unwanted bid to shake up a company? What they appear to be doing now they could have done a long time ago. Only now are they apparently dealing with longstanding issues that are restricting growth and holding back the share price.

The great news is we can all learn and improve our business by using the Unilever experience. Here's what you should do, no matter how big or small your company is. Create a crisis by dividing your executives into two small teams. One for attack and one for defence. The attacking team will highlight all those areas where the company is weakest.

The exercise will identify investment ideas that haven't delivered, that you're too proud to scrap. "We'll give it one more year." Underperforming brands with declining sales. Low-margin products that don't compare favourably with competitors. Overseas territories that have never hit budget and are now a drag on the P&L. Subsidiaries that lose money and the occasional vanity project that adds no real value to the business.

Private equity firms are expert at identifying what a company needs to do to shake itself up. They employ risk capital for high returns. They identify underperforming businesses ripe for improvement. It's a peculiarity that in these companies the management can't see what the private equity guys see, or can, but have but failed to act.

I know the owner of a highly successful restaurant group. He says, "there's no steady state; you have to treat every day as a state of emergency". This has served him well. Take little for granted and use some of your time to identify performance improvement.

The away-day home team need to provide some very quick and tangible reasons why things should be left as they are. The attack team have highlighted perceived weaknesses. You'll already know what they're looking at.

The second part of the day should be spent agreeing that the identified areas of weakness should be finally dealt with. Now. Of course, there will be complications, perceived difficulties and challenges to take on board. Of course there will, which is why they've probably been in the too-hard basket for so long. You'll need to agree deadlines, responsibility and resources.

But dealing with these things will be liberating. It's like putting off going to the dentist. You know you should sort out that niggling tooth before it gets worse. You don't; it gets worse and you go. But it doesn't hurt as much as anticipated, it takes less time than you thought and you realise you could have sorted it a lot sooner. Your corporate challenges are no different in many respects.

If you clear the decks of the things that are holding you back, you can look at improved performance, often in a relatively short period of time. It's a case of finding the courage to challenge and change and not being too proud to resist doing what others see as obvious. And then you have more time and resources to do the things to grow the business. Which tends to be much more enjoyable.

The Monday Revolution (you can start on Monday)

1. Review and agree the critical business lines. Put a monitoring system in place. Make sure the alarm is switched on.
2. Ensure essential suppliers can continue to supply. This means understanding their financial business model and accounts.
3. Learn from the problems of others. Look at how they handled the situation and use their experience.
4. Recognise there is no steady state. You are expected to have a plan even though the crisis may be less than obvious.
5. Always turn up and do what's required. Going missing is a human response. But as the leader that's not an option.

6. Behave as a predator would and make the changes and improvements to your company before they do.

Chapter 21
Deft decisions
Evidence-based. Always.

Cutting through the noise when making decisions can be challenging. The pressure to act immediately can be overwhelming. And in such situations, emotion can often overrule facts and experience. We can be pushed into setting aside the available evidence that would help us decide on executing a more effective course of action.

A guiding principle of *The Monday Revolution* is using evidence to make better decisions. How do we really know? This is a question I've found myself increasingly asking, particularly when there are difficult, similar or less clear-cut choices to be made.

A paramedic dealing with an unconscious person needs to find evidence very quickly to make a split-second lifesaving decision. A company manager will mostly have more time, but the principle of reviewing the available facts to reach the best possible course of action remains.

In many instances there will be an in-built tension. The cognitive response to just getting on with it versus the lengthy time that gathering evidence may take. In these situations, gather what you need to apply early judgement. Will delay make the decision more difficult or complex? Or could it buy you time for a better outcome? This could be an important call to make.

Of course, the evidence itself needs to be challenged. There may be many sources available but the quality of each will no doubt vary. These will need to be weighed up and judgement applied, before being taken into account as part of the decision-making process.

In many situations the evidence is ignored or discredited because it fails to confirm the preferred course of action. Noisy people with strong opinions can crowd out better thinkers who have less confidence to share their views. Yet these silent voices could provide valuable insight. Ensure they are given the encouragement, space and protection to be heard.

I was in a room with my team, doing a deal to buy another business. Surrounded by bankers and lawyers from both sides of the transaction, all having a commercial interest in seeing the contract signed. By acquiring this company, we could remove duplication and create a larger, more efficient organisation.

At one point a banker suggested I should ignore the evidence we had diligently acquired regarding the amount of cost savings (a key part of the deal rationale) and announce a far larger number to the shareholders and media. "David, you should be looking at £13M in savings not £10M, it will be very well received." I replied we had no evidence beyond £10M and anyway it wouldn't be on his shoulders to make it happen. He said, in front of a crowded room: "You're not being brave enough." However, the evidence didn't support his cavalier advice and I wasn't grateful for his unnecessary public put-down. I took that into account several years later when I was part of an interview panel reviewing his job application.

Sometimes insisting on reviewing evidence can be miscon-strued by others. Particularly those who like to back up their decisions after the event. More often than not, the way forward isn't always clear. Choices avail themselves and these need to be weighed up and judged according to the evidence. Which itself requires judgement as to its relevance and robustness.

Here's one way of thinking about it. In every minute of the day we subconsciously process evidence. It's a cognitive behavioural response to our immediate circumstances.

We recognise danger and avoid crossing the road in the path of heavy traffic. Then again, we might further weigh up the evidence and arrive at a different conclusion. The vehicles are slow moving. If I walk in front of them, they're likely to see me and not speed up and I can navigate my way across. That's more risky than standing still. But I've assessed the evidence, which includes my previous experience of crossing this busy street, and I'll step out…

Becoming a revolutionary for evidence-based decision making is one of the easiest and most effective ways of improving all aspects of your life. This is no exaggeration. Applied to both business and personal choices, developing the ability to stand back and seek out information and weigh up facts will mean you reach better decisions. For the most part, this is better than just jumping in or relying on hope!

As an advisor at a management meeting I listened to a discussion about whether people in the company understood the ambition and purpose of the organisation. There were mixed views. Some managers felt their teams were up to speed. Others were less sure. I offered to conduct a sample of interviews to establish the facts. Armed with the evidence, the management team were able to make an informed decision about how and what to communicate, when and to whom. A good conclusion.

But many companies would have progressed on the individual assumptions of their managers. Without the facts. "I don't think we need to spell it out; people know what's going on." Often those who speak loudest in such circumstances prevail. This is not always good.

Evidence can provide counterintuitive information. In such circumstances it's particularly important the gathered evidence has an agreed integrity from all involved. Asking current buyers may be more robust than a general market research survey.

At the product development meeting of an online consumer food business that sells high-quality meat, it was suggested the company should start selling fish as well. Some thought this was a pretty crazy idea. The reputation the organisation enjoyed stemmed from its excellent traceable, sustainable meat supply. Why jeopardise the reputation of the business with a new supply chain for a product range the customers weren't expecting or indeed asking to buy?

As an online business with many regular shoppers it was decided to ask them, as part of a wider customer survey, whether fish would appeal if offered for sale. The evidence was overwhelming. Now they ship fish to the majority of customers, as well as meat.

Without doubt, one of the most subjective areas where evidence is regularly pushed aside is that of people (see the earlier People section). A trap we all fall into. Making judgements based on first impressions, likeability and anecdotes served up as facts. I suspect on more than one occasion you'll have wondered how someone you've just encountered, in a senior position, managed to achieve such lofty heights of success. Well, you know how it happens – no real evidence was involved!

Joe was a popular manager with his peers, team and bosses. Personable and always positive. Good to spend time with in and out of work, he was an obvious candidate for promotion and a directorship was available. The company, quite rightly, had a process for deciding such matters and besides there were other people to consider. Although he was the favourite and very much the people's choice, Joe missed out this time. Why? Because when the evidence of past performance was diligently examined, Lucy's track record beat him hands down. Although a lot less high-profile and not such an obvious personality, her measurable achievements could not be questioned. Joe understood and the company made the right, if not the most obvious, decision. I've worked in organisations that would have slipped up here.

The Monday Revolution requires a habitual shift to mandate evidence-based decision making. This may sound contradictory to our mission of simplification and expediency. But it's not. Effective evidence-based processes enable better decisions to be made more quickly. Why? Because confidence levels increase with better, more successful results. The doctor confidently prescribes a drug because previous patients have been cured. You recruit a new executive having applied a proven process that tested their skills and reviewed the evidence of previous achievements.

I've encountered much resistance to evidence-based decision making. Although it's hard to argue with the logic, many people much prefer to rely on their experience, instinct and gut feel. Some see the use of evidence as a way of others deferring decisions, putting off what seems to them as the obvious choice of action. These are valid considerations but do not in themselves justify ignoring information that would provide the necessary answers to help us make the right choice. It's important that you are a strong and resilient proponent of evidence-based thinking and actively promoting it in your business.

How do we really know? It's a good and significantly important question to ask your colleagues before a decision is finally taken.

The Monday Revolution (you can start on Monday)

1. Try introducing a culture of evidence-based decision making (assuming you don't have one). The best reference point is www.cebma.org
2. Use examples of where you currently use evidence and apply the principle to other areas.
3. In meetings where you make decisions, ensure the sponsor can back up their recommendation with evidence.
4. If you do the above, you will change to an evidence-based culture, over time.
5. Always ask: "How do we really know?"

Chapter 22
I want one of those!
Acquisitions

Mergers and acquisitions, or M&A if you want to sound like you know your way around the corporate world of deals. You've a vision or plan that you believe is needed to grow certain or all parts of your business. And that requires buying another company to succeed.

Or maybe what you do is becoming irrelevant, the customers are starting to drift elsewhere, and you need to become more cutting edge before the wheels fall off. Perhaps building or buying your way into an adjacent market is what's needed to solve the problem.

Starting from scratch is hard. Evidence suggests that great businesses do this, and the best businesses are the ones you build yourself. But inevitably this will take time and that might not be on your side. Or perhaps you've created a company to buy others. "Buy and build" as it's known. Sticking lots of related businesses together, cutting the central costs and creating something of scale. Or buying unrelated companies from different sectors, just using combined scale for central purchasing and cheaper head office costs.

These conglomerates were fashionable for many years and the USA is still home to two of the world's largest, Berkshire

Hathaway and GE. Both are a collection of businesses with little in common other than ownership.

There are many models and reasons why M&A activity takes place. There is a multibillion-dollar industry, which includes banking, lawyers, corporate advisors, PR people and a slew of others there to encourage and help. They don't get paid until you complete a deal. They also don't carry the can if it doesn't work once the acquired company is in your hands. That's down to you – their job was simply to get it over the line and get rewarded.

If you're in charge of a business, you have responsibility for what's known as capital allocation. In other words, where do you put the company money to best effect? Internal projects or outside acquisitions? Dividends? Or a bit of everything? In the rapidly moving digital world I allocated money to a large in-house online team far too early and under-invested in other projects.

In trying to build a digital company in-house I found that the risk of allocating potential profits to the project was increasingly risky and unsupported. So we just played at it and the lack of serious commitment meant we didn't get very far.

On the other hand, we made many acquisitions buying radio stations, as we couldn't make them ourselves due to limited airwaves and the highly regulated environment we existed in. These, for the most part, were simply integrated and often we were bringing greater resources and opportunity for most of the people who joined our group. Of course, not everyone will remember it that way and I can think of more than one occasion where our clumsy handling caused problems we could have anticipated and prevented.

Every study I've ever read on M&A says all the value that's created resides with the seller. The acquiring company will often be in a well-orchestrated auction for the prize. And mostly will overpay as a result. This is known as the buyer's premium, the extra you have to pay for the privilege of complete ownership and control. In many instances it takes many years for the purchase price to be earned back by the acquiring company.

Commonly, the identified synergies don't materialise as generously as predicted. Or perhaps the acquired company dragged sales forward and cut costs, such as marketing, to improve short-term performance. This should have been picked up in due diligence of course, but sometimes isn't seen as a major issue in the heady rush to win the prize. In a competitive pursuit you see what you want to see.

In service companies that just rely on people for their product, advertising agencies for example, a different type of deal often takes place. The acquirer pays an initial sum and the rest of the purchase price is paid over a period of years providing the previous owners have stayed around to deliver. To some extent this mitigates the risk in that the acquirer isn't paying for earnings that fail to show up.

Fair enough, but you may end up owning a company that has underperformed. But I suppose you haven't paid for it in that regard. Better than paying a full price upfront and ending up with a company that is worth a lot less at the end of the day. I had a narrow escape in that regard, courtesy of Richard Branson, Chris Evans and the private equity giant Apax. My boss at Capital left halfway through the deal and I took over. Looking forward to buying Branson's Virgin Radio and becoming the proud owner of the Chris Evans Breakfast Show I didn't anticipate events would result in the deal being upended.

But that's what happened. Chris told everyone we'd fire him and pleaded on air for someone else to step up. Barbara Manfrey from Apax decided to back Evans and the existing management and Branson took their money not mine. As he said to me over breakfast at his Holland Park house: "As you've been referred to the competition people the deal might never happen. And I like Chris Evans, he's a great fit for the Virgin brand." Well, I couldn't argue with either of those points so that was more or less that. All that remained was to tell everyone, that would be my board of directors, advisors, team, staff, media, shareholders and many others, that our number one strategic target was now off-limits.

However, with hindsight I think Branson did me a favour. We were paying far too much money because in that era radio was extremely overvalued. And the cultural fit would have been very difficult to manage. They didn't want to be sold by Branson and certainly not to their closest and most despised competitor.

Much further down the road we made much smaller better-value purchases. Richard gave me and my customers upgrades on a Virgin plane and Chris bought me a few drinks in his newly acquired Hampshire pub. In the end it worked out for everyone. Apax sold the business to SMG, the Scottish TV group, and made Chris a very rich man. Sadly, SMG sold it for much less – the bubble had finally burst.

The tempting expediency of deal making, fuelled by an industry of self-interest, isn't going to disappear any time soon. The harsh truth is companies need to grow. But building things yourself takes commitment and skills you probably don't possess. Many try to emulate the start-up culture within their own organisation. I've seen it work but it requires a very different mindset. So, if your core business is dwindling and you haven't the in-house skills to build it yourself, acquisitions are probably the only answer. Other than put your company up for sale. Fine, if you're a fast-growing former start-up, but less easy if you're a mature company looking for a home. No easy answers to this one.

The Monday Revolution (you can start on Monday)

1. Growing your company should not rely on ad-hoc acquisitions, however tempting.
2. Advisors have a transaction-driven agenda. Mostly they do not have your best interests at heart. They carry little responsibility for the deal beyond the initial transaction.
3. Unless your company is designed for acquisition – such as a private equity business, whose sole remit is deploying risk capital – recognise the risks involved in what can be unfamiliar territory.
4. Obtain examples and case studies of where acquisitions in similar situations have worked well. Employ the same principles and metrics.
5. Don't underestimate the challenge of integrating systems and cultures. Employ expertise to help before the deal is done.
6. I'm not saying don't do deals. But I've had my own failed experiences and the media constantly reports many more. Just be careful.

Chapter 23
Buried treasure

Discovering a new business in your business

Coming up is a true story of a guy who started from scratch, built a company and discovered buried treasure in the organisation he'd founded. Because when you put interesting, curious people together and create somewhere that encourages ideas and discovery, great things happen.

Link that up with ambition and commercial nous and there's a chance you'll find gold. I'm increasingly convinced that within many companies lie great undiscovered opportunities. You just need to create an environment where they can show themselves.

Whether you're a private or public company, partnership, at an early stage or longstanding, your business is valuable. For most of us that's something we aspire to increase through good decision making and hard work. Every company owner and investor that wants to sell would like a top price and there are many ways of valuing a business.

So how do you ensure your financial model is attractive? And what can you do to improve your chances of attracting investment or a successful sale at the right price? Whether it's your personal shareholding or those belonging to other investors.

To grow your company there are basically two ways of course. Organically or by acquisition. The former may appear harder, take longer and is not without risk. Buying an existing business eliminates the development uncertainty and may provide instant revenue, profits, synergies and cost savings. It's quicker too. Just remember executional and integrational risk and the common danger of overpaying – as described in the previous chapter.

As an either-or, how do you choose? Often larger companies acquire because they have the need for immediate growth. Usually, in spite of their size and resources, they recognise they lack the skills to create and build in-house. The culture can't support the investment risk and potential failure. So, they buy.

Evidence suggests this can be a difficult thing to get right. Most acquisitions favour the acquired. This is because they secure a premium price for their company. In other words, more than it's probably worth, meaning the acquirer is generally paying too much. This is easily done. I am more than guilty of convincing myself and my colleagues that in a competitive situation we can more than justify the price. We'll take costs out, drive sales harder and bring our superior management skills to bear.

The evidence is somewhat different. Most acquiring companies would be better off leaving the money in the bank. Or doing as Andy Brown, an extremely successful self-made multi-millionaire once said to me: "The best businesses are the ones you build yourselves." And he should know.

So how do you begin to do that? I've already said it's not easy for an established organisation to succeed. Some create a new team, physically separated, funded and tasked to deliver new initiatives. Others try creating R&D departments or putting money into a venture capital fund to finance other initiatives and hold a stake they can eventually turn into ownership.

All of these can work, and you need to decide if you should do anything at all. If your core business has good growth potential, stick with that and don't invest in something that will impact your bottom line and cash flow. However, most companies need to grow and often that means looking outside the primary business. Your current model may be great for now but not fit for purpose at some point in the years ahead. In fact, it definitely will not be.

Because sometimes you have to accept that what you have is not really good enough. In spite of prudently controlling costs and generating revenues, the financial characteristics are such that you'll never realise a high price.

So how about looking at it a different way?

It's possible that within your current business there are opportunities to build something new. A product or service where the financial structure and possibility to scale would attract keen buyers and a high valuation. Or if that's of little immediate interest, one that would provide the growth the company needs. Who wants to run a business that's run out of steam? All you have to do is find it.

Often, it's as simple as rearranging or repurposing what you're already doing. Perhaps by revamping your business model, moving from one-off payments to recurring revenues, for example. But that's what you should be doing anyway, constantly looking for better ways to get things done. Or sometimes by doing something more extreme as happened to this exciting company run by Paul.

I was at a wedding reception seated next to Paul, whom I'd heard of but never met. His reputation was one of a guy in a hurry. A big hurry. From leaving school he'd built a small but fast-growing business but lacked the experience (he was in his twenties) to know the best direction to go in. Although it was a social occasion our mutual friend thought it would be a good business discussion (Paul doesn't really talk about anything else) so that's what we did.

Paul's business generated sales leads for clients by telesales marketing. As a salesman himself, he'd built the business with two friends from scratch. The early years were hard and with little funding the company lived hand to mouth trying to pay their small number of staff. But as time went on, the business began to grow, client numbers increased and they had to hire more people to service the customers. The profit margin was pretty good and they could pay themselves a reasonable salary.

They outgrew their offices and moved to larger premises. By now the company was turning over several million and employed over 300 staff. The cost base continued to go up but that was fine because so did the revenue. Then one day out of the blue, they were asked if they wanted to sell the company.

They met with the prospective purchaser but came away disappointed. Although the business had grown quickly and made reasonable profits, it was much less valuable than Paul and his fellow founders thought it should be. Why would that be, you may ask?

The simple answer was the short-term nature of their sales. Clients required a sales campaign to generate leads for their business that would last a few days or weeks but no longer. Consequently, Paul's company required a fat pipeline of opportunities to ensure they could pay the bills and grow the business. Of course, some clients returned but it was mostly impossible to predict.

When asked to forecast revenues for the next year or two it was pure speculation, based on history, because more than six months out there were no confirmed customers. This is why their business was worth less than they thought – the "quality" of their revenues was relatively poor in that there was no future certainty. Furthermore, if the revenues grew as they had in the past, this would require more people, so with little scalability the margins would remain static.

However, it wasn't all bad news. Buried in their tech department was a software product that was to transform the business. Phil was the IT director, an ideas kind of a guy, who recognised a possible opportunity and convinced his colleagues to provide a small development budget.

The invention was a simple product, but hardly used or offered to clients – mostly its existence had been forgotten. The basic idea had been to inform organisations how people had used their company website, which parts they'd dwelt on and which parts they'd ignored. Although you couldn't identify the person you could identify the inquiring business in many instances. This information allowed companies to improve their online presence and target particular sectors and organisations. It also provided insight into what people were really interested in, so they could develop new products accordingly. Of course, Google already provided a version of this, but it was by necessity generic and not as bespoke or as helpful.

Paul decided they could be onto a winner. A natural online extension of their lead generation products. It could be sold by their existing sales teams to current customers and a lot more besides. But Google Analytics offered a free version, so why should anyone buy theirs? A good question and at that point the project would have been shelved by many others. But Paul's team decided they could create a nimbler user-friendly relevant product. Sure, Google might just improve theirs and blow them away. But they gambled the company wouldn't be bothered by a very small business and Google were unlikely to resource a payment and account management system to support it.

I have to say, this for me was a significant risk. In my experience avoiding getting on Google's radar, or indeed any tech giant, is usually a good idea. Until you want to sell to them. With their resources they can swamp your idea and blitz your customers almost at the press of a button. Luckily, Paul isn't averse to danger, so we ploughed on.

The motivation to succeed was overwhelmingly compelling. Instead of building a cash-hungry lead generation business that required more and more people as it grew, they could create a scalable software company. This was would have far more value per revenue-generated pound than the existing company. Why? Because success would mean a customer base making regular payments and a product with global appeal that could be marketed anywhere.

They did a test selling the software on the basis of a month's free trial and then a low-cost subscription. The tried and trusted "fremium model". They retrained part of their existing sales team and sold it over the phone and online.

The cost was development, sales and account management. A highly scalable product with predictable subscription revenues. Over time it was easy to forecast the customer drop-off rate, which meant even if they didn't sell a single further subscription their revenues were predictable for several years.

Paul was no fool. He understood that the company now had two related businesses but in order to create the most value for him and his colleagues he needed to take one more important step. He separated the two companies entirely. Not just by separate accounts and board structure. Physically too by moving into another building. And then into the USA.

A good example of a Monday Revolution principle. Acting decisively now. It would have been all too easy to find reasons for the businesses to remain integrated, sharing costs and inter-dependencies. But there was a bigger prize at stake.

They sold the original lead generation business for cash and became multi-millionaires as a result. They built further related products and the subscription revenues continued to flow. Not surprisingly with a high-margin, scalable business, with strong predictable revenues, buyers will soon come looking.

I'm convinced that nearly every business can revamp, discover or create a scalable business if they really want to. You don't have to wait for a disappointing low-ball offer to get going.

I worked with Paul and his colleagues for several years. I helped Paul identify the opportunity. I explained the higher values attributed by buyers to recurring revenues. I even identified the buyer for the lead generation business. Paul and his colleague paid my fees, bought me a dinner and rewarded me a small commission on the sale as a thank you. They are both still in their thirties and I'm convinced will build and sell the much bigger company when they feel the time is right. The lead generation business might not have been the best from a valuation point of view, but it's made them both very rich.

The other company is now international. Paul spends most of his time in the USA where it generates millions of dollars in revenue. This company will eventually sell for many, many millions. Paul and his friend built both these organisations from scratch. The companies have no debt and they both own all the equity. It can be done!

All from a recognition that their current business wasn't really quite what they wanted but could fuel the growth of something that already existed as a piece of early-stage software. Buried treasure.

The Monday Revolution (you can start on Monday)

1. Start with what you're already doing and identify the things you believe are unique to you.
2. Ask your customers or clients what you could do better or supply what you currently don't.
3. Delegate some of your current people and resources to the new project.
4. Tech is where you create scale. This is the holy grail. Repeat predictable revenues. What are you doing that could be adapted to fit this model?
5. Delegate a very senior executive (probably you) to lead the initiatives.
6. When you've found it, test it yourself. This is so important. Personally sell it to customers like Paul did.

Chapter 24
Who's your friend?
Partnerships and pitfalls

Hanging out with the "right" people can pay dividends. There's a halo effect on both parties. Partnerships can result in great things happening and there are plenty of them around. Data-sharing deals, joint ventures, brand tie-ups and associations.

Great companies manage their brands extremely well. A strong brand will endure, take hard knocks, recover and allow its values to endorse other products. Intel told everyone that there was "Intel inside" and it became a mark of quality and endorsement for many. And that's just a single example of how to do it. You'll think of many more.

There are many factors we should take account of when building our business and setting out to capture market share. Here's a case study based on personal experience featuring British Airways and Marks & Spencer. But it could be almost anybody. It's a lesson on what happens when you bring two brands together and how you could make it work better. At least, better than my own experience.

Hard-earned reputations are easily lost. We all know that. There are many aspects within our control to ensure we maintain and enhance how others see us. Yet sometimes it's too easy to grab an opportunity without thinking about how things might turn out. A cynical colleague of mine said that partner-ships only work until one side has learnt all they need from the other. Once they've acquired the knowledge, they become far less committed. There is a lot of truth in this.

But if you're under pressure for profitable sales, it can be easy, or convenient, to set aside the dangers of what might lie ahead. Or worse, to ignore how the reputation of a business partner will impact on you if they slip up. Because you'll be damaged by association, even if the situation was not of your making. If you hang out with bad people their reputation will tarnish you and your business will suffer, be in no doubt.

These two British companies decided to work together. Both have had moments of great glory and hold a special place in the hearts of many. Yet both have occasionally struggled to hang on to their enviable past reputations. One has suffered from numerous strikes and operational issues, the other has been in a constant state of turnaround.

Outsourcing is a highly efficient way of providing prod-ucts that you would struggle to make yourself. Catering is an example where finding an expert company to supply and deliver what you need can be an important commercial decision. Most businesses outsource in-house food and drink to someone else who knows what they're doing.

Taken a stage further, you can use their brand as something to make your own even more attractive and compelling. But you need to be careful. One and one can make three but also one and a half.

When British Airways hooked up with Marks & Spencer to exclusively supply their food on their European routes it encountered a challenging start. BA no doubt wanted to make money on their in-cabin catering. Just like a number of their leaner competitors. Quite right too. However, BA were about to present their customers with the option of paying for M&S snacks as opposed to previously providing meals for free, in that they were previously included in the ticket price.

BA had probably decided they're not a catering company and consequently didn't make a great job of it. But customers get hungry and competitors seemed to make it work.

Teaming up with a company with a great reputation for food and selling theirs instead made great sense if the right deal could be done. Find the right brand, sell more and gain a great reputation for in-flight service was no doubt the rationale. Although I have to say at this point, I have no idea how the deal was done, so what follows is pure conjecture.

After all, what a great proposition from BA. The contract would be worth millions and whoever won the race would be selling huge volumes to thousands of people.

I imagine the response at M&S was pretty euphoric. A company under pressure finding a new customer to sell their products across the skies of Europe. After what had been a fairly gruelling few years, this would provide a potential fillip to the share price and a boost to morale.

And the deal was sealed. M&S would be an exclusive supplier to BA. In return they would receive a multimillion-pound contract and feature heavily in both in-flight and external marketing. The perfect British fit.

Unfortunately, my personal experience of this exciting new deal fell a long way short of expectation. In the rush for sales it would appear that M&S have some way to go in ensuring their high product standards can be met at 37,000 feet.

On a trip back from Italy, my wife Alison was served with a hot savoury product. Impossible to eat because it had congealed within the packaging and appeared extremely unappetising. Looking around, we could see that other people were looking rather disappointed; it really wasn't just us. The cabin crew swapped it instantly, very much giving the impression this had happened a few times before. But two reputations had taken an instant hit. M&S, because the product fell way short of what we experience at our local branch. And BA for serving food that couldn't be eaten.

No doubt things will improve. They both need to work really hard at that before long-term reputational damage sets in. Particularly as up until the M&S deal BA had supplied catering for free.

I agree that this simple tale sounds like a petty and inconsequential experience. But it's a useful metaphor for what seemed like a good partnership that encountered early problems that should have been thought about.

I'm pretty sure the right questions weren't answered properly from the start. How will our product perform from cold shelf to aeroplane oven at high altitude? Will the cabin crew be able to ensure each is delivered in pristine fashion or will we just be sharing a poor catering reputation with each other? Whatever was intended, it wasn't the outcome we experienced; I'm pretty sure of that.

Of course, we must assume that everything was thoroughly tested before it was launched in-flight. Maybe, then, it was just down to the training and execution. Whatever the issues, something in the end-to-end process failed.

At Capital Radio we struck a deal with Disney to launch and run a new digital radio station on their behalf. At a critical stage of the final negotiation, the UK management told me the company president, Bob Iger, wanted to speak with me.

"Sure. I'll happily talk to Bob, where is he?"

Cindy Rose, UK country manager: "Tomorrow, he'll be in his private jet flying from Burbank to New York. We'll connect you."

And that's what they did. At the allotted time, Bob came on the line along with lawyers, Cindy and her team.

"Hey David, thank you for making the time for this call."

I love the way American business culture requires a super-friendly start to any conversation. My guard was up.

The essence of the conversation was that the House of Mouse had never handed over editorial responsibility to a third party. And Bob wanted to make it clear if we played explicit adult music lyrics on the radio station to his audience of under-twelves we'd be for the high jump.

I made a couple of points. First, we have rules and regulators in the UK who are far more stringent than the USA. Second, we have a brand to protect too and if Disney stepped out of line, we would take a similar view.

"Bob, we're the company that holds a regular party in Royal Hyde Park for a hundred thousand people. It's a joint venture with the Prince's Trust and Prince Charles always attends. Hopefully that will provide some comfort that we know the value of a brand relationship and how to behave."

With that, Bob was happy and the deal was done. A successful partnership ensued for "Capital Disney" and both sides bene-fitted. Cindy told me later that no one had ever dared to suggest to Bob that Disney might screw up! Some weeks later, Bob was in London and we had a few drinks and a laugh about that.

The agreement really did a great deal for Capital. As a commercial venture not too much. But as an association with a company known to be highly selective in their partnership dealings it was an immense endorsement.

The Monday Revolution (you can start on Monday)

1. When you lend your brand to someone else be sure you can control the quality and service. Don't risk your reputation on their delivery.
2. Don't sacrifice reputation for the lure of short-term revenues and profits.
3. Their reputation will stick to you and yours to them. When two companies come together, it is the reputation of the worst that prevails.
4. Do sufficient testing, due diligence and build in safeguards.
5. Make sure the contract has an exit clause for underperformance.

Chapter 25
Three-year plans and other nonsense
The tyranny of prediction

In the past UK companies were often accused of not knowing how to plan for the future. In contrast, stories abounded of Japanese organisations planning their progress for a hundred years or more. I have no idea whether this was true or not, but the success of Japanese industry was nailed to a meticulous long-term view of the future.

Perhaps the tipping point for UK companies was to realise that making it up on the hoof was not a guarantee of success. And so, the three-year plan was born. Like me, you'll have encountered many occasions when this cornerstone of UK business culture raises its head.

Chairman: "When's our strategy day taking place?"

CEO: "October so we can shape our thinking for the financial year."

Chairman: "I think the board would find it useful if the divisional heads presented their three-year plans and you and the finance director bring them all together for

the company. I think our advisors should be there too,
efficient way of keeping them in the loop."

Is this a good idea or a fairly pointless exercise? The answers
depend on a number of things. If the company uses three-year
planning as a regular management tool to plot progress and
benchmark decisions, then it's arguable it could be time well
spent. But if that's the case, everyone would already be regularly
updated, so spending a day hearing what they already know
would be a pretty poor use of time.

But most companies, certainly in my experience, only
prepare three-year plans for occasions such as a strategy or
board away-day. The chief executive returns from the board
meeting to inform his team that a considerable amount of their
valuable time will be absorbed preparing for the big day. Most
will dust off last year's PowerPoint as a start and leave the exercise as long as possible before they get going.

Is there any value here? Arguably the exercise of a three-
year plan helps executives take a future view that will impact on
day-to-day decisions.

"Our three-year plan relies on purchasing storage space
to scale the company, perhaps we should be buying
more capacity than we need right now?"

Of course, that may be a prudent decision, but it may result
in paying for unnecessary capacity and that will affect margins
and profits.

The three-year plan provides comfort to the board that the
company has thought matters through and that there's a basis
for the decisions that will need to be made. Although it's the

tradition for most companies I've ever been involved with, I've personally become increasingly convinced of its diminishing worth. We should consider planning *The Monday Revolution* way to ensure positive practical results.

I recently discussed this with an executive who works for a fast-growing tech company which you will have heard of.

> "When I first joined, we had a three-year plan but then we ditched it. Why? Because we can't predict the next six months let alone three years!"

His company now operate a three-month rolling plan.

Frequently, consultants and advisors encourage organisations to build a plan out of what the company is now and what it should look like some years further on. Often, in order to encourage greater accountability and improve personal responsibility, each executive is required to write their own three-year plan. I have become increasingly persuaded that this, in many instances, is a fairly pointless, time-consuming exercise that fails to deliver the desired objectives.

As my converted friend said:

> "If you ask them to plan their activity for the next three months, share it with their colleagues and account for what they've done each week you'll see better results."

So, what to do?

Having no plan looks like incompetence. If you don't know where you want to get to, how will you know when you've arrived? Many organisations like to add their company ambition to public material, presumably to convince others and themselves that there is, in fact, a plan lurking in the wings.

> "Our ambition is to be recognised as the leading/go to/pre-eminent delivery company offering mobile solutions to all our customers."

I asked the marketing director to explain to me what exactly that meant. She said: "Well… it could mean we appear first in the Google search rankings." We agreed it could mean a great deal of different things, or indeed not much at all. Unless it's attached to something concrete, it's meaningless. But as so many companies tend to do this, we mostly don't really expect it to be defined. It's only awkward people like me who make the challenge.

I have my own planning ideas. They may not work for you, but they may be at least worth consideration before embarking on an expensive and time-consuming exercise. In the interests of full disclosure, you need to know I like to attach measurements and timings to most of what I do. Others may disagree but I don't think I'm obsessive. Years of being told things that people really believe, that turn out to be factually incorrect, has formed my thinking.

It's pretty simple really. What do you want to be by when? If you're driven by size, market share, margins, number of customers, staff welfare, diversity or a host of other metrics, start by agreeing where you are today. The baseline.

Decide where you want to be and what you will need to do to get there. If you must use three years, break down the actions and resources into small steps. If a three-month plan, make it weekly and a three-year plan monthly. Personally, I would break down a three-year plan into weekly actions. Starting now.

And then do two more things. Assign personal responsibility for each task and meet weekly to check progress, make changes, review assumptions. If the meeting only lasts 10 minutes that's fine. It's about ensuring you're all doing what you agreed to do. And if competitors disrupt your assumptions, you're well placed to respond.

If you're a start-up, you'll be familiar with this approach. Because it's dynamic and fits *The Monday Revolution* plan. If you're a large company with layers of process and a bureaucratic approach to business, this system is particularly for you. But no doubt you'll need to jump through a few hoops to make it work.

I'm not saying don't have a plan. It's more to do with why you need one and what purpose it serves. My friends would tell you I'm the least spontaneous person they know. I always want to know what the plan is. Where are we meeting, what time and who's booked the restaurant? I hate aimless wandering trying to decide if we go here or go there. A plan puts a stake in the ground, allows you to put the right things in place and provides a better chance of getting the desired result.

Let's agree there are definitely many reasons why plans make so much sense. Plans are about the things that need to come together to achieve the desired result. And it's easy to argue that a result is more likely to happen with a plan in place than a series of unconnected actions and a bit of luck that might get you there.

In your life, your business or whatever, the right plan will help you achieve. It improves the odds of success. But plans come in many guises, shapes and sizes. What do you need? A plan for today or five years? How can you ensure your business can translate plans into actions? Who is accountable and why?

I've met many, many people and looked at countless plans, from the hopelessly naive to the over-complicated, with more moving parts than a Rolex watch. I've seen some good ones too and made investments on the basis of what I've observed and discussed. Whether multinationals or exciting start-ups, I've always looked for early evidence of success. And reviewed the management as best I can to try to ensure they are capable of doing the tasks in the plan that are critical to its success.

The one thing all plans have in common is they are at best a hypothesis. Until they've happened in real time, they represent our best guess of how we would like things to turn out. We're forced to make assumptions, sometimes based on prior results and sometimes guesswork, because often we have little or no evidence to support our views.

The underlying assumption in this book is you want to make progress because forwards feels better than backwards. So, what might work for you or your business? How can you determine the best route to success with a plan or plans that are aspirational but achievable? What evidence can you gather?

Many years ago, I was in New York and spent some time with Keith Reid whose name might not be immediately familiar to you. Keith is a lyricist. He writes words for songs and has enjoyed global success with the band he first started writing for many years ago. That band was Procol Harum and Keith wrote all their lyrics including the iconic song "A Whiter Shade of Pale". Keith is a modest, unflashy kind of a guy with a great sense of humour and, not surprisingly, a way with words. It wasn't easy; he didn't have the music industry contacts and needed to build relationships from scratch. I asked Keith, who has enjoyed fantastic royalty streams since the early days, what his plans were for the week ahead. He replied: "No idea, I've never planned much of anything!"

That stuck with me. The possibility of success without a plan. I'm pretty sure Keith didn't have a plan to be a lyricist either and write the words to one of the most familiar songs on the planet. As he told me recently, at the time he didn't really know anyone in the music industry. But his natural talent, ambition, self-belief and the circumstances prevailing at the time aligned and he's never really looked back. Most of us can't rely on that, so we make plans to try to improve our chances.

If you're running a business, you need a plan. Not least because it's expected. If you're like Keith with a regular income and nobody to account to that's fine. But that's not the case for most of us. As a manager of a business, perhaps small and looking for investment or a global corporation, when asked or challenged to explain your plan the answer can't be "we don't have one of those".

Yet once our aspirations are baked into an Excel spreadsheet and distributed to others, the plan becomes a matter of record to be judged by. And here lies the problem. Without a tacit understanding that plans need to be regularly revisited and adjusted, they can become a dangerous weapon, especially in the wrong hands.

I was introduced to Sarah who was concerned her business was on the slide and was determined to do something about it. The company had some great assets, but they needed investment and a new sales and distribution plan. Her paper magazine needed to move on from print media to new digital channels where the readers had migrated to in large numbers. All sorts of ideas and options were discussed, and a business plan was prepared for the board to approve.

After much debate the plan was signed off and Sarah got her hands on the money. So far so good. But compared to delivering the business plan, that was the easy bit. The assumptions Sarah and her team had made proved to be wrong, at least in the short term. The decision to invest the money had not been an easy one for the board to make. The idea had competed with other options, backed by individual board members, who were less than supportive of the majority decision to back Sarah.

Now the gloves were off. The business plan versus actual performance provided the dissenters with the evidence they needed to torpedo the idea. Sarah's business found itself increasingly under the microscope and not in a good way. Targets were missed, the business required more cash and the model remained unproven. Let's come back to Sarah and what might have been done differently, shortly.

Investment always requires sound reasons and they come in the shape of the good old three-year plan. One year is too short and five years is too long so three years it is, in most instances. I've had much involvement in writing three-year plans for companies seeking investment. Because this is what investors expect and frankly, their money is needed. Year one is a loss, year two break even and year three a profit. The revenue lines will be highly aspirational and the margins significant to reinforce the illusion of a high-growth company.

The good news is nobody really believes it. Investors recognise if half that growth is achieved, they'll be pleased. Yet the game needs to be played because anything less than a steep upward curve looks lacking in aspiration. It gets played out time and again. Smart investors look for validation of product, achievement to date and evidence of what's happening now, not three years out.

Plans are necessary, logical and can make sense. But in the wrong hands the idea can suck the life out of everyone involved.

Michael is the leader of a successful partnership. Although very accomplished, he's not always as confident as he might be. He tends to latch on to the last idea someone says. At a partner meeting he told the story of a recent encounter with an opposite number. This guy, in order to encourage greater accountability and improve personal responsibility, had told each of his people to write their own three-year plan. Michael wanted his team to do the same. I persuaded him that this was a pointless, time-consuming exercise that would fail to deliver his desired objectives. As I've already said: "If you ask them to plan their activity for the next three months, share it with their colleagues and account for what they've done each week you'll see better results."

How best to prepare, write and execute a plan that has a fighting chance of happening? As discussed, the longer the plan the least likely it is to get done. My preference with three-year plans is to break them down into very small steps and hold those steps to account. On the basis the plan will result in a different set of priorities and actions you should start now. Business guru Peter Drucker observed that plans only succeed when they degenerate into actions.

Plans should be reviewed every three months, assumptions revisited, new evidence presented, and numbers changed to reflect the new reality. Sarah's plan should have had health warnings all over it. The short-term goals should have been achievable to provide confidence to her supporters and cynics. If you're in new territory, plan a much shorter timeline. No problem painting the big picture a few years out. But the real work should be in validating the new idea and investing short-term money to prove the concept. I've personally never struggled to raise company money for an idea that appears to work.

Ensure the plan has the right measurable outcomes. It needs to be commercially driven, whether you're in HR, finance, marketing, sales or somewhere else. Share your plans and results in order to hold yourself and your colleagues to account.

The Monday Revolution (you can start on Monday)

1. Honestly appraise the business today with your chosen metrics. The baseline.
2. Decide what you want those metrics to be at a given point in time.
3. Work out interdependencies (what relies on what?) to set priorities.
4. Build a plan which requires personal responsibility for what needs to happen by when.
5. Have a very regular meeting to review assumptions and stay on track.
6. Keep tasks within reach. Small steps are far more effective than big leaps. No time like the present.

The Monday Revolution conclusion

One step at a time

A t a gig in London, Huey Morgan of the Fun Lovin' Criminals challenged the audience to consider spending life in a more rewarding way. In fact, he said: "You're all going to fuckin' die, what are you going to do between now and then?" After these words, Huey reinforced the message with another question to drive it home: "What are you going to do when you leave the room?" I love that question.

What are you going to do now you've read this book?

The point of *The Monday Revolution* is that it contains a lot of information about things you can do, actions you can take. It's over to you now. Based on this book, can you create a plan? Can you take what you've read, understood and think: "That's me, that's what happens in my organisation and maybe, just maybe, there's a way we can do things a bit differently and bit more effectively?"

There are over a hundred action points in this book. Applying them all, in the context of your own working life, will prove challenging. But some will be easier to adopt than others. Start with those to create momentum, credibility and impact. Prioritise the rest. Set yourself some deadlines to help stay on track. For each task to complete, ask if not now, when?

As you've invested some time reading this book, let's ensure that it's been well spent. Taking just one thing and successfully applying it could significantly change your prospects, enjoyment, satisfaction and business!

Some of you may have read this book cover to cover. Others may have dipped in and out, perhaps finding reassurance in something you already knew, or maybe disagreeing with some of the things you've read. Likely some of both.

But, as importantly, you may have found some answers and ideas to the everyday challenges encountered as part of the working week. Ones that could be solved, streamlined or completely disregarded.

What is the most important task to revolutionise this Monday?

I want to make sure you've taken the opportunity to change things for the better. I realise this book will be read by different people, in very different roles. Some actions will appeal specifically to chief executives of organisations. Others to those just starting out. But that's fine because the advice is hierarchy, gender and age neutral. No one is too important or too junior to find better ways of getting the important things done.

Everybody can have a Monday Revolution.

Viva la Revolución! An Afterword

Prof. Cliff Oswick – Cass Business School

The Spanish phrase *viva la revolución* is typically translated as "long live the revolution". It is seen as a celebration and endorsement of the revolution. Just like the Spanish Revolution, *The Monday Revolution* is, in my opinion, worthy of celebration and I would certainly endorse it. It is packed with really good practical advice. It is informative without being "preachy". That said, if you are reading this afterword you have probably already read the content of this book and formed your own opinion. The purpose of this afterword is not to offer gushing praise or try to convince you it is a good book. I want to say something about enacting the revolution.

According to *The Urban Dictionary*,[1] *viva la revolución* is not simply uttered in praise of the revolution. It is to be shouted as a call to action: "to start a revolution and begin to fight against an establishment". This is in line with how I see *The Monday Revolution*. But the enemy is not "the establishment". It is an internal enemy. We need to challenge our established ways of thinking and fight against our taken-for-granted and

---

[1] An online alternative dictionary, www.urbandictionary.com

ill-informed assumptions about business practices and popularist management wisdom.

Assuming that you feel that the book has merit, I want to offer some brief advice on how you can "fight the good fight" and move forwards with your personal Monday Revolution. As David points out in the concluding chapter, there are over a hundred action points in the book. He suggests that it is important to prioritise and take one step at a time. This is extremely sound advice. I want to offer two further suggestions to assist you in your revolution.

First, having highlighted areas you wish to tackle based upon salient advice in the book, you need to tentatively experiment with the new processes and new behaviours required. In most instances, things are unlikely to go smoothly straight away. I would therefore encourage you to actively embrace a process of "critical reflection": a systematic, retrospective consideration of an event or events. In my opinion, the best technique for this is the *Reflective Cycle*,[2] which involves six relatively straightforward steps: 1) description (what happened?); 2) feelings (what were you thinking or feeling?); 3) evaluation (what was good/bad about the situation?); 4) analysis (what sense can you make of the situation?); 5) conclusion (what else could you have done?); 6) action plan (if it arose again, what would you do?); and then back to step 1.

Working through this process has been shown to be an effective way of identifying and successfully embedding good practice.

---

2   A process developed by Graham Gibbs in his book, *Learning by Doing* (1988).

Second, *The Monday Revolution* is a fantastic book to help identify key areas for personal improvement in business life. In this regard, it focuses on the "content" of the revolution. In order to leverage the excellent advice offered and optimise your personal revolution, I would recommend complimenting it with a book that offers exceptional advice on the "process" of making a revolution happen. The book I am thinking of is *Atomic Habits*.[3] There isn't space here to go into the detail of the book. Suffice to say, it offers excellent, clear and accessible advice on how to build good habits and break bad ones. In particular, it shows how to make tiny changes to create life-changing outcomes. If you are serious about working on your personal revolution it is worth reading.

The advice presented in this book by David is analogous to the advice offered by a very experienced and talented personal trainer. It represents an important and powerful starting point. You wouldn't expect to walk out of a gym induction or an introductory personal training session fit. Fitness requires you to enact the good advice you have received. It requires commitment, dedication and perseverance. Equally, this book is a manifesto for your revolution. It is not the revolution. It is a call to action. Your revolution is now in your hands. The hard work begins now. It requires commitment, dedication and perseverance (along with some prioritisation, planning, critical reflection, and perhaps the development of "atomic habits").

Good luck - *viva la revolución!*

---

[3] This highly influential, bestselling text is written by James Clear (2018).